OVERCOMING ALL ODDS

I Overcame Poverty, Illnesses, and Abuse

Ron N. Reel Ph. D.

Paperback: 978-1-964035-67-3
eBook: 978-1-964035-68-0
Library of Congress Control Number: 2025901888

This is a work of nonfiction.

SWEETSPIRE LITERATURE
— MANAGEMENT —

FOREWORD

This is the story of my life from birth, through high school graduation and the death of my mother, to my enrollment at Trinity University. The "Postscript" continues my story up to the present. With God's help, I survived poverty, several serious illnesses, and physical and emotional abuse from my father. I hope that this book will inspire you to meet head on any problems in your own life and to have greater empathy for those who are working hard to surmount their own difficulties. I needed the help of a loving mother, facilitative teachers, encouraging clergy and their congregations, and a number of friends I made along the way. They were there for me, and others like them will be there for you.

The accuracy of any memoir depends upon the memory of its author. In those cases where I had not been physically present, or could not remember specific details, I had to rely on the memories of witnesses or on family lore. Many of the events and actions in this memoir took place between 1966 and 1968. Flashbacks to earlier times are woven throughout the story. Recalling events from over fifty years ago is difficult and I have found that the saddest and most hurtful events are often those most easy to remember. I have learned to forgive, but that does not excuse the fact that certain actions should have never taken place. I realize that reality rests between truth and perception. My memories are my perceptions and therefore my reality. Others may remember the same situations differently.

As best I could, I tried to avoid two temptations: exaggeration and omission. If I say the lights in our house were turned off for a few days, they were off for a few days. Saying they were "off for a week or two" might have added drama to my story, but I stuck to the way I remembered it. Some of you may wonder why I describe the physical abuse my father committed against my mother and myself. I have tried to tone down the description of the acts themselves, but I remember these events vividly and they had a profound effect on my life. They had to be included in my memoir. I have changed many of the characters' names to avoid any embarrassment they might experience from the publication of this manuscript. Because this is a memoir, I kept my parents' names and twin's name. All three of them have passed away. I have also changed the location and names of schools I attended, as well as the names of my teachers and mentors. I have done my best to hide the true identity of people I met along the way. Should similarities arise, it is only coincidental and no one person should assume they are that person. In fact, to make the narrative easier to follow, in a few situations, I have combined the actions of two or more different people into the actions of one.

Both my mother and father spoke with strong dialects, reflecting their backgrounds in Oklahoma and not being educated properly by credentialed teachers. In some cases, e.g. "ya" for "you" and the omission of a final syllable, "gonna" for "going to," I report the sound I heard. Most of the time, however, I let them speak General American.

I wish to thank Carolyn Inmon and John Arrijuria for proofreading and editing my manuscript. I want to give a special appreciative acknowledgement to Dr. Hal Bochin, not only for being the major editor, but for being my writing coach. His contributions, suggestions, advice, and friendship allowed me to complete this project. This story of how I overcame poverty, illnesses, and abuse would never have become a book without them collectively, and Dr. Bochin specifically. Any remaining errors are mine alone.

CHAPTER ONE

My identical twin Donald and I were born on June 2, 1950, in a government camp, a step or two higher in quality than the one John Steinbeck wrote about in *The Grapes of Wrath*. Both of my parents were itinerant farm laborers in central California. My parents already had six children (three boys and three girls) before my twin, and I were born. Momma gave birth to us in Selma, California. Our house was a small shack on Seventh Street, separated from the other government homes by railroad tracks. In this little farming town, there was no good or bad side of the tracks. Both sides were filled with impoverished people, struggling to make a living for their families.

We were born at home because we were too poor to have health insurance; besides as Aunt Dovie (my mother's favorite sister) said, "Your momma already did this six times before." Momma had sent the older kids, who were still living at home, out for the evening to stay with other aunts and uncles. Aunt Dovie always claimed that I was born at five minutes to midnight and that Donald was born five minutes after midnight. If this were true, my birth date would have been June 2 and Donald's June 3. Momma did not want any of the problems or questions different dates might cause and insisted we were both born on the same day. She won the argument and our official birth certificates say we were born at five minutes before and five minutes after eleven on June 2.

Momma, Augustine Reeves, had been born and raised on a Cherokee Indian Reservation in Bell Star Canyon, Oklahoma. Father, Willie Harlan Reel, was reared in Porum, Oklahoma, a small town not far from the reservation. They were married in 1935. Father was twenty-one and Momma was eighteen. At that time neither of them could read nor write.

After marriage, Father worked most of the time in the coal mines of Oklahoma. Many of our relatives on both sides had strong ties to the mines. Father's dad and one of his brothers had contracted "black lung" because of the hazardous and often unregulated mining of this type of coal. Momma was afraid Father would become another victim of this terrible disease and tried to convince him to move to California where many of her family had already settled.

The Reels are a very large family. Father had eleven brothers and sisters. Most of them migrated to Arizona. But Father told Momma that he thought the weather there was too cold in the winter and too hot during the summer. Momma had thirteen brothers and sisters. Most of them had left Oklahoma and traveled to the Fresno and Clovis areas of California. Some of them had been a part of the "Dust Bowl" migration leaving Oklahoma with the hope of getting rich. History suggests that only a few of those original settlers from Oklahoma found financial success. Many of their children or their grandchildren, however, did make it out of the agricultural fields.

By the time I was six or seven, we had moved to Clovis, California. The houses on Park Lane all looked alike. From the outside of the houses, one could not distinguish differences between the numbers of family members living there. The houses had one or two bedrooms. Occasionally there was a third bedroom. All had only one bathroom. The average home size in the United States during the 1960's was about 1,300 square feet; and by the 1970's, it had grown to almost 1,500 square feet. The homes on Park Lane were mostly around 500 square feet.

Many of these homes were not finished construction. They did, however, have utilities. The design was very simple and functional. You entered the living room through the front door. Immediately to the left or right side was the bedroom. The bathroom occupied the other side. You walked through the living room to the kitchen. There was usually a back door at the end or to the side of the kitchen so that each dwelling had two exits.

If there were a porch, it was usually located at the front of the house. It was small, and in most cases, did not keep rain from hitting the front of the house during the winter months. The houses were small by any standards. Most of the bedrooms sheltered at least two people and usually three or four. Some families had all of their children sleeping in the bedroom while the parents slept in the living room or vice versa.

Most of the houses had fences of some sort. These fences were not designed to keep people out. They were used to distinguish the actual boundary of the property for the owner or landlord. Most of the fences were wire and could be jumped over at will. None of the fences were more than a few feet tall. Some of the lots without fences had five, six, or seven of these homes, side by side. They shared an area where the children played when the parents were not using it for a parking lot. Wealthy farmers owned many of the houses where we lived. Rents ranged from $25 to $50 per month for the right to live in a home with electricity and running water. One must remember the farm laborers did not make much money. During this time the average farm laborer made $2.00 per day. When both parents worked that gave them $120.00 monthly. This economic issue forced most of these families to put their children to work. They labored before or after school, on weekends, and during the summers. Some of the children would be pulled out of school to work when their parents needed extra money.

There were a few times when my father was unable to pay our rent on time and this led to our having to move out of our home. I was only in the fourth grade, but I remember trying to figure out why our family moved so many times. We were living in our fourth house on Park Lane in Clovis. I am told it was the seventh house we had lived in since I was born. Little did I know there would be more than twice that number before I was a senior in high school. We seemed to move without much notice. We would be told by one of my parents, usually Momma, that we had to move and within a few days we would leave one house for another, often in a different city.

Momma was the parent responsible for making sure the financial obligations were paid in a timely manner. When they worked, both Momma and Father were paid by check. Because Father could not read nor write, Momma always signed his name on his check for him. Neither one of them had a checking account with a bank. Momma would go to the bank where the check was drawn or go to the grocery store at the end of our street and ask for cash. Banking was different then; it was much easier to cash checks. Father would always pay bills with cash. Momma would count the precise amount, give it to Father, and Father would then deliver that amount to the landlord, utility company, or grocery store. Momma told us the bill paying would be much easier if she were the one delivering the money to the various places, but Father felt it was his responsibility, as the head of the family, to show the outside world that he was the one taking care of the family. Momma usually went with him to the various places, handed him the invoice, told him how much was owed, and made sure he had the correct amount of cash to pay it. He would then go inside with the invoice he could not read, hand the invoice to the person responsible for collecting the payment, point to the amount due, place the cash on top of the invoice, and wait for the receipt. He was very good at hiding his inability to read, and no one ever questioned him because he always had exactly the correct payment in cash to pay the bill. Momma was instructed to wait in the car or stay outside while Father skillfully acted as though he were in control of the situation. He would come back to the car and ask Momma to verify the payment had been made correctly.

Sometimes when Momma was ill and could not leave the house, after she signed his name on his check, he would go to the store or bank and get the cash himself. I would hear them arguing when he would get home that some of the money was missing from the amount the check stub said he had been paid. Father always had an excuse about why he was short. They included: his needing to purchase something for his work, buying something for himself, the check stub had the wrong amount on it, and many times, he simply said he must have lost the money. The lost money excuse caused great arguments between the two. The discussion would often escalate first to loud voices, and then to noises that sounded like hits, moans, and eventually Momma crying.

One night I heard Momma say to Father, "Mr. George came by today and said you did not make the rent payment." Father raised his voice, "He wasn't home when I went to pay and so I left it with his wife. I will clear things up tomorrow."

"Bill, he says you did not leave any money, and he wants us to move out," countered Momma.

"I will clear things up tomorrow. Let me take care of this. Ain't none of your concern," he snapped.

"I gave you the exact amount to pay him. Did you spend or lose the money?"

Father was now enraged that he was being challenged. "I know you gave me the money and I left it for him. Maybe his wife kept it for herself." I heard him hit the wall with his fist.

Momma spoke slightly louder than he had, "If you paid him, then we can prove it. I have a payment record I keep. On that record is the date I gave you the cash and the amount. You show him our record. Now he says he wants to meet with you tomorrow. It will be just like going in to pay any of the bills."

Father was not going to have this type of interference. "Let me take care of this and you stay out of it. I am the man, and just because you can read and write some, don't mean I can't handle this here situation. I knowed what I did," he said.

"Well, do you want me there with you tomorrow when you meet with him?" Momma asked.

"No! I can do just fine myself," responded Father.

"Let me give you this payment book so in case you need to use it you can. Just pull it out and give it to him and tell him right here is my record showing each month's payments and the last one shows this month was on time," she advised.

"I don't need that. I'll just talk to him in my own way; man to man," he stated.

"Take it with you and use if you need it," Momma said as she left their room. I moved away from their door and jumped back into bed. She did not notice me; or if she did, she did not draw any attention to me. I thought I should keep an eye out the next day for the meeting Father had with our landlord. It was about 4:00 p.m. on Sunday afternoon when I heard Momma call for Father to go to the door to see Mr. George. I knew Father would not talk to him inside the house. He would not want anyone to hear their conversation. I headed outside and positioned myself behind one of the large hedges so I could see and hear what happened. Father and Mr. George came out of the house and went about ten feet from the front door. Father spoke first, "I done knowed why you are here. I can explain if you give me a chance," he said.

"Bill, there is no explanation. The agreement we have is that rent is paid on time. I was told by your last landlord that you had a history of missing a couple of payments before I accepted you. If you remember, we talked about it and you told me that would not happen again; so, I gave you a chance," explained Mr. George. This was the first time I had heard we had been late with our rent before. I hoped Father would take out the payment book Momma had given him and use it to show Mr. George a mistake had been made.

"I don't know what to tell ya." You wasn't home so I left it with what I thought was your wife," Father stated.

"Bill, what day did you make the payment?" asked Mr. George.

"It was Saturday. Saturday about noon. I came home from work during my lunch hour," explained Father with clarity and detail.

"I knocked on the door and nobody came to the door at first. I recounted the money to make sure it was all there. Got my payment record right here." Father handed him the payment ledger Momma had given him.

Mr. George stepped back and said, "Bill, that is impossible. I was the only person home on Saturday, and I did not leave because that is the day all of the renters drop off their rent payments. You should not lie to me." Mr. George must have been mistaken. Something caused me to move from the shadows of the shrub and move toward Father and Mr. George. They both noticed me at the same time.

"Mr. George, Father does not lie. If he says he made the payment, then he did. Perhaps you left for a few minutes and while you were gone, your wife got the money and forgot to tell you. Have you checked with her?" I asked. Father looked shocked that I was interfering with their conversation.

"Boy, you stay out of this! Get back in that house. I can handle this here. I am sorry Mr. George my boy has said anything. Ronald get the out of here now," he shouted. I retreated to the side of the house. I could still hear the conversation.

"I am sorry he butted in Mr. George. I will deal with him later. Now, can I make up that payment in the next couple of weeks by payin extra. I must a just thought I went by ya house," he pleaded.

"We both know you did not make the payment. Because you lied to me, I can no longer trust you. You are not a man of your word. I am going to have to ask you to leave the house. I expect you to be gone within three days and the house to be in the same condition it was when you moved in. Is that clear?" he asked as he turned and walked away.

Father had been caught lying. I didn't understand why Father would lie to the landlord. I can only imagine he was going to see him and ask for an extension. Instead, they argued. He went back into the house. I heard him and Momma begin discussing Mr. George's visit. They were both using loud voices.

A few minutes later he slammed the door and left for a few hours. When I got the nerve to go back into the house, Momma was sitting at the kitchen table with a bag of ice over her black eye, which she said was caused when something from the dish cabinet had fallen and hit her. Father never talked to me about the incident. Momma told us that night we would be moving again. We moved back to Selma.

Most of the farm workers had limited, if any, formal education, no medical coverage, older cars that had serious problems, few household appliances, few televisions, and many hand-me-down clothes that were shared with family members or refurbished clothes that had been given a new life by sewing creativity.

We lived in a mixed racial community with Caucasians, Latinos, and African Americans living side by side. I do not remember any violence, hate, prejudice, or distrust among the people living within this community. I don't remember any family members having issues with the color of skin of anyone. We never locked doors. In fact, we called each other family. I thought I had many cousins, aunts, and uncles of many colors. It was much later in life I found out about the types of racial issues that confronted some parts of the United States.

Perhaps it was the lack of television or the fact that most people in our community did not have access to newspapers that contributed to my naivete about racial tension. The families I knew stood together and helped each other as needed. Our address did not dictate our family values, goals, or aspirations. We were a community of family members. Our address did not rule our family.

CHAPTER TWO

If one could play sports, there might be a chance for leaving the agricultural fields; at least, for the time spent on the "playing" field. We all knew of people who had made it out, only to return a year or two later. For the non-athlete there seemed to be no chance of moving from the fields of the central California valley. Their field held whatever crop needed harvesting. The days were long, and the hours were full of physical pain, suffered from sun, rain, bugs, or pesticide spray. The long hours provided time to dream about a job that would take them inside.

The contractor, or boss, was responsible for making sure his workers completed their tasks in time to bring in the harvest. There were rules regarding age, start and end times, safety of working conditions, amount of pay for the workers, living conditions, break times, and sanitary conditions, which they were supposed to follow. If one were to point out a problem in this area, however, the boss would likely claim, "If you don't want to work, I can find somebody that will." Some of the field hands did not know or did not honor the rules, regulations, and constraints imposed by the state and federal governments. I remember a time when Donald and I were picking potatoes. Momma and Father were working at a different location far away from us. They were on the east side next to the main highway. They could not see us. Each of us had an area in which we were responsible for picking the potatoes and putting them into a gunny sack; when it was filled, we had to take it to the boss, have it weighed, and then get an empty sack and return to pick more potatoes.

That morning, an adult male who was working beside us for some reason decided to take some of our area of potatoes each time we would move to a new spot. I remember asking him why he was not going in his allocated direction instead of ours. When he would not stop intruding into our area, I started picking in his area. He was not happy with me "stealing" his potatoes. After I stood up to him and explained that he was doing the same thing to us, he stopped picking our potatoes. I learned early that one had to stand up to people who were not fair to all. The demands placed on many of the farm workers were often, hard, and brutal.

One of the fastest sprinters in the history of Clovis High School had an opportunity to leave the fields. He was determined to get out of the farming environment. His running prowess got him into junior college, but his academic shortcomings prevented him from getting into a four-year school. He was forced to return to Clovis. I was determined that I would never let academic shortcomings prevent me from leaving this environment.

Somehow, I knew my life would be different from those around me. I knew I was not to continue the family "field worker" tradition. Each of my older three brothers had transitioned into field worker contractors and provided as best they could for their families. Each had gotten married before the time they should have graduated from high school.

Without formal education or specific career technical training, they had few choices available. All my older brothers were forced to work for different farmers throughout the valley.

I knew my field would be neither athletic nor agricultural. I was a good track long distance runner and thought about possibly going to college on some type of track scholarship. None of my older siblings had gone to college. Of the older six, only Hannah had graduated from high school. She had married someone in the Army.

I was told it was foolish to think I had a chance to make a living by running. Family members warned me of a future injury and noted my history of illness that might derail my plans of escape. I was not even the best runner at my high school, so I was easily convinced my future in professional track and field was just a dream.

Our track and cross-country coach was ranked fifth in the national rankings in the mile. He had just graduated from an Ivy League college and this was his first teaching job. None of us knew why he had chosen Clovis, but we were really glad he had. He didn't just coach. He ran with us at each practice. He was a part of our team. Actually, as I look back now, we were all a part of his team. He too was training for his competitions. Coach, as he had us call him, used us to help him train while he used himself to help us train. He would have each one of us run a 440-yard lap against him. None of us could run fast enough to beat him, but after his running two or three laps against fresh and energetic runners, he was pushed to keep his pace up to beat each new runner. He was only five years older than some of the seniors. He in some ways served as a big brother role model.

I did not like working outdoors in the fields. I had two bouts with rheumatic fever as a child, and my heart could not take the heat when it came to work outside in the fields. The temperature was over 100 degrees almost every day during summer months. Rheumatic fever had also left me with a heart murmur that could only have been completely controlled with special medication. Momma and Father never seemed to have extra money for such luxuries when I was younger. It would take a miracle to heal me.

I was really good at reading and understanding concepts when called upon by my teachers to explain the major divisions and thesis statements of covered material. I could memorize the work the teachers would give as assignments before any of the other students. I could even recite the forty-eight most common prepositions. One of my eighth-grade teachers, Mrs. Green, had an assignment to memorize and recite them to the entire class. I was the only one that did it perfectly for her class the very next day after it was assigned. "About, above, against, along, around, at, below, beyond, ...etc." I won't take the time to share all of them. You can look them up if you want. You may want to memorize them for yourself. It is a great conversation piece. It also serves as a great way to spot grammatical errors like dangling participles. Education is the best way to climb out of poverty. I learned that early in my school career; my twin Donald never did.

When we were youngsters, my twin and I thought of ourselves as a team. We dressed as closely alike as possible, down to the number of buttonholes on our shirts. If you saw one of us, the other was nearby. If one of us liked a certain type of food, so did the other. We loved doing the same things. When we went to kindergarten, the teacher thought it would be best to place us in the same classroom, so we would not suffer from separation anxiety. As it turned out, twin girls were already in the class and we became friendly with them quickly. They were the first twins with whom we had contact. When Donald and I got to third grade, the teacher asked our parents if she could separate us because Donald did not speak up much during class and I did not do many physical activities on the playground. When the teacher would ask any type of question like, "How many people in our story actually went on the vacation?" I would answer immediately, but if Donald were asked the same question directly, he would say, "Ask Ron, he does our talking for us." Donald was very shy and felt uneasy when called upon to say something in a situation that involved more than the two of us, or people other than family members. He loved math. I hated it. I loved writing and reading; especially reading aloud. When other kids wanted Donald to take a stance or make a decision on his own, I tried to protect him by using humor. We would always confer, but I would be the one to give his answer.

Once we were separated in school, Donald did not start speaking out as our teachers expected. Instead, he would not say anything at all during classroom discussions. He also started showing signs of what we now know to be a learning disability called Attention Deficit Disorder, but at that time, educators thought he just was not capable of learning the material on his own. They would call him stupid or say he was working below level. We would study our vocabulary, grammar, and math in the evenings. Both of us would understand the material when we were at home; but, by the time we got to class the next day, Donald would not be able to spell, recite, nor do the math that we had learned the night before. Somehow it just disappeared.

It is hard for me to remember my earlier life when I did not have some type of illness. I was the one who was sick most of the time. I always had a sore throat during the winter months. My adenoids and tonsils were infected at the same time. The tonsils are the two small glands on either side of the back of your throat; sometimes referred to as the adenoid tissue. Enlarged tonsils and adenoid tissue are usually referred to as tonsillitis and adenoiditis. They can be caused by infection or allergy. The adenoids and tonsils are supposed to work together to trap germs that come into your mouth and nose. The adenoids are located high up in your throat behind the nose. When they do not function properly, they grow in size and do not do their job. These enlarged adenoids and tonsils cause symptoms that include sore throat, difficulty in swallowing, earaches, problems breathing through the nose, headaches, and blocked stuffy nose.

My doctor told us how large and problematic my tonsils were in comparison to those of normal children. He compared mine to Donald's. His were smaller and he never seemed to get sick. My swollen adenoids would almost touch each other. The constant dripping from the adenoids area kept my throat moist, and this allowed bacteria to form. The initial treatment of tonsillitis or adenoiditis for children is medication. I spent many days in bed following the doctor's orders of resting, drinking fluids, rinsing my throat with warm salty water, and taking overthe-counter pain relievers that Momma and Father purchased at either the local grocery store or sometimes at the drugstore. By the second bout during the winter months, we progressed from over-the-counter medications to antibiotics. I was to take these drugs for ten to fourteen days. By the third bout each winter we would progress to nasal steroids and saline spray to help reduce the inflammation.

Every winter the doctor would recommend surgery to remove both the enlarged adenoid tissue and my tonsils. Each year we waited out the time, medications, and prayed because we did not have the funds to have one or both taken out. Surgery would have resolved the medical problem, but because they were not removed, each year the treatment available to us could not stop them from becoming more inflamed and less resistant to any type of antibiotic medicine. The constant deterioration of these two natural blockers allowed germs to form almost at will and each year I seemed to have more bouts with this illness than ever before. My older brothers and sisters teased me relentlessly during the winter months with a saying they repeated over and over, "Ron has Tonsil and Adenoiditis. They would always laugh after making these remarks.

Donald once told me a secret, "If they think I am dumb or can't figure things out, that is fine with me cause I don't like school and going there has not gotten any of our older brothers and sisters anything." I remember the night he said that, I prayed that God would take some of my learning skills away from me and give them to Donald so he would not have to struggle so much. Unfortunately, things got worse. He stopped doing his homework all together because he felt he would not remember most of what he had learned when he returned to school the next morning.

He had been smoking since we were in kindergarten. He would swipe cigarettes from Father or find a used cigarette butt and relight it. By the time we were in the third grade, he was smoking daily. Father would give him a cigarette and dare him to smoke it. Father thought it was funny to see him smoke and he wanted others to see how cool his kid was. He did not discipline him in any fashion. Father smoked and he was pleased that Donald wanted to be like him.

By the time we were eleven, I noticed a lump or thickening located at the side of my breast. Donald did not have a lump. There was a redness to my skin covering. It was quite sore, and within a couple weeks the lump was beginning to show when I was just wearing a T-Shirt. Donald was concerned about my condition. He told me that his initials were DR which stood for Doctor! He said, "I think you should go see a real doctor because I don't like when you are sick. We can fight and make fun of each other, but I don't want anybody else to make fun of you because of your lump." In his own way he was trying to protect me. I went to the doctor. He explained that every person is born with a small amount of breast tissue and that the breast tissue consists of milk-producing glands called lobular ducts that carry milk to the nipples. This takes place in men and women. During puberty, women develop more breast tissue causing their breasts to become larger.

The doctor wanted to run blood tests and perform a biopsy to see if my lump was cancerous. His concern was that if it were cancerous, the tumor would spread (metastasize) to nearby tissue and then spread to the lymph nodes or other parts of my body. The biopsy would determine whether the cancer was benign or malignant. Most people don't know about male breast cancer disease because it is so rare in men. The results came back showing it was a ductal carcinoma. That means it was cancer that began in the milk duct of my breast. The results proved it malignant. He removed the breast tissue during an office visit. Other than the scar on the right side of my chest, there is no other reminder that I had cancer. The breast returned to its normal size.

When we got to the eighth grade, Donald was in jeopardy of being held back because he could not pass the test on the Constitution required for graduation. Finally, after he failed to pass it six times, the teacher asked me if I would stay with him and help him with the answers. I will never forget that event. We were told to come back to the classroom at the end of the school day. The teacher handed Donald the test and informed us she was going to the office, and when we finished the test, we should let her know that we had left the test on her desk. Her departing words were, "Ronald, I expect you to read the questions out loud for your brother and you both can talk through the answers. Make sure Donald answers enough questions correctly to pass." Once she left. I read the questions aloud. Donald had his pencil and paper plus his answer sheet. I did my best to get him to come to the correct answer; however, when he didn't know the correct answer, I told him how I would answer it. There were 100 questions and the passing score was 70%. When we finished his score was posted by the teacher as 75%. I don't know why this teacher had us complete the assignment in this manner. She told us she did not want Donald stuck in the eighth grade and driving himself to school like one of her other students, who had been in the eighth grade for three years.

Father always complained about my studying too much. He did not see value in education. Our eighth-grade graduation occurred when we were living in Fowler. We had moved to that town at the end of September so we would be there during the preparing and picking of the orange groves. We were living in two onebedroom shacks side-by-side on one of the farms. It was one of what I called our crop rotation moves. We moved from area to area depending on the crops and the farmers for whom Father and Momma worked on a regular basis. In all, I attended three different elementary schools in three different cities, two junior high schools in two different cities, and four different high schools in four different cities.

When we were in the eighth grade I was selected to be the student commencement speaker because of my grades and an audition. The school gave me a certificate as special recognition at that graduation ceremony. When we returned home, Father said, "I don't know what all that fuss was today. After all that commotion and you up there talkin, Donald got his diploma before you. So, it didn't make any difference cause ya both got the same kinda paper; but he got his before you!"

By our sophomore year, Donald had for all intent and purposes stopped attending school. He was skipping school and working in the fields with Father. He was a chain smoker and drank beer and wine on a regular basis. We were still expected to share the same bed, but I could not stand the smell. For half the year I slept on the floor.

A memorable moment came toward the end of our sophomore year when I was running long distances on the track team. I had a visit from our new Assistant Vice Principal for Discipline. He was shouting, "Reel,

Reel, Donald Reel, I need to see you right now!" At first, I did not hear him. I was running sprints. One of the other students got my attention and gestured for me to look to the bleachers. I saw Coach making his way to him. By the time I arrived, he was explaining who I was to the administrator. I heard him say, "Donald Reel cannot be participating in sports because of his grades and attendance. He is a truant, and I won't have him representing this school." I was horrified. I knew the vice principal had mistaken me for my twin. I interrupted, "I am Ronald Reel. I have a twin named Donald. I think you are looking for him." He started to move closer to me. He put his hand on my shoulder trying to turn me to walk with him away from the track.

"I can assure you there must be some mistake. I have one of the highest-grade point averages of all the students in my class. I have never failed any class and don't think I have any issues with attendance either," I protested.

"I know my job and do it very well. I am sure it is you I want," he said as he started walking and pushing me from the bleachers back to his office. Coach was trying to explain to him about the mistake. "Sir, you are wrong; and I can prove this if you just give me a chance," Coach said.

"You may want to back off and let me do my job since this is your first year and you don't have tenure," the administrator said in his most authoritative voice. I walked with him back to the office knowing I had done nothing wrong and he would soon be given the evidence to set me free. "Place your fanny down and listen to what I am going to do about your insubordination and your truancy." I watched him as he pulled documents out of his desk and place them in a stack before him.

"You need to know I am the boss here. I have all the power. You are going to do what I tell you. We are going to suspend you again, and we are going to do our best to prevent you from ever returning to this school." I let him complete his rant.

"Students like you damage the reputation and the integrity of this school. I have taken it on as a personal duty to free us from people like you. You will take these papers home to your parents. You probably don't have a parent who can read these documents. So, if you are as bright as you say, read them out loud to your parents. Either your mother or father will sign them if they know how to write. One of them must return with you in the morning. Tomorrow we will officially remove you from our campus. You will not be allowed back during school hours or during any activity sponsored by the school. Do you have any questions as to how we are going to proceed?"

I wanted to laugh at him because he was so far off base. I did, however, want to respect his position. I took a deep breath and as calmly as I could, I answered him, "I realize you are new and there is a long history of my twin and myself at this school. We are as different as night and day. His name is Donald, and I am Ronald. If you can ask your secretary to come in here, I am sure between the two of us we can convince you of the mistake that has taken place. People can make mistakes. The ladies in the office, however, have had to deal with us so much, they can distinguish between the two of us. Please, will you ask Mrs. Payne to come into your office?"

The vice president felt he was on solid ground and he would call her into the room to prove he had not made an error. As Mrs. Payne arrived, she looked at me and said, "Ronald what are you doing here?" He looked up. Before he could make any comment, I said, "I have been confused with Donald, and he thinks I am not eligible for sports. Can you help me out?" I asked.

She spoke in a very caring and controlled manner: "Evidently you have not met the Reel twins. One, Ronald, is a model student while one, Donald, is rarely here and when he does make a guest appearance, he does not participate in most classes, can be found out in the smoking field (as we call it), and has no aspirations of graduating. You do have the wrong twin."

"Are you sure this is not Donald? I am rarely wrong," he said to her. She looked at me and then back to him.

"I am sure."

"Well, then, I want to see both you and your brother in my office in the morning so I can see for myself," he told me.

That meeting never happened. When I got home with the paperwork and the news from the school, Momma, Father, and Donald decided the drama I was somehow causing was affecting Donald in a negative way, and they did not want his reputation as a truant to spread. They decided he did not have to go back to school.

Donald had not been attending school on any regular basis. He would leave in the morning and spend most of his day visiting with other delinquents, going to stores, hanging out around town, and smoking as often as he could get cigarettes. Now he was going to have to be more accountable. He would be working side-by-side with Father. He promised my parents he would work each day in the fields and find out how to complete a high school equivalency either during the summer or in the evenings. Donald was very happy he had been released from his school torture. After all, he was already "smarter" than both of our parents because he had falsified his school attendance for the entire semester. In his mind, he could control his own destiny.

I returned to school the next morning as instructed. I did not have my twin beside me. In fact, neither of my parents accompanied me. Momma called the main office and informed them that Donald would not be returning to school and asked them to send home any forms she needed to sign to make this happen. I was told at the front office I could go straight to my first period class. I thought the decision my parents had made the night before was wrong. Donald could, if required, do his homework and attend classes, and earn passing grades. There were other students far less intelligent and less capable of performing academic tasks than Donald who were being forced to get their high school degree by their parents.

I had difficulty sleeping that night. For some reason, my parents believed I had caused the crisis that resulted in Donald being thrown out of school by my staying after school to practice with the track team.

Father asked, "Why can't you just go to school and come home when it is over? No, you have to be out there tryin to fit in with them rich kids."

Had Donald been responsible and attended school regularly, we would not have found ourselves in this situation. Donald always played his "I cannot remember things, so why try" card since early on in elementary school; but he was an expert with this excuse now. I believe that he never forgot all of the material he had been assigned; he remembered just enough of what he wanted and or needed to know. It was easy for him to tell people he did not remember. He didn't have to do more than what he wanted to do; and he got away with it.

About three months after this incident Momma and Father decided Donald would be better off living with a more affluent relative for a while. My twin went to live with relatives in Pittsburg, California. They told Momma and Father that if they were to get Donald all the help he needed; they would need legal custody of him. I believe that is what happened.

These generous people thought they would give Donald some needed attention and help him by purchasing some reading programs and paying for tutoring. They felt this would allow Donald to return to regular school. They thought they could make a difference in his life and help Momma and Father with this problematic teen. I had no idea this was going to happen because it had not been discussed with Karen, Frances or me before they arrived. They showed up just before Easter and took him from our home to theirs.

Donald never returned to live with us. He called home each week (when our phone was working) bragging about their new color television, new car (which they let him drive), the allowance they provided for him, and the fact that he was planning to go into the Army by Christmas or, at the latest, the following year. Evidently, they told him if he passed his current classes and made up the classes he had failed, they would give him permission to enter the military. We were only sixteen, but they, had gone with him to the recruiter's office and lied about when he was born, telling them he was about to turn eighteen. They signed a document falsifying his birthdate. Donald had left home just as Momma's heart problems began getting worse. We twins were separated and would never be reunited.

CHAPTER THREE

It seems like it was yesterday, but it was almost five decades ago. The year was 1962. I was twelve years old. Although we were the second set of children to be raised by our parents, our family had not progressed much financially or educationally. None of the six older children lived at home. They had married young and now had children of their own. I was only four years older than my oldest nephew. The pain and suffering of poverty had not gotten any better for our family. Both of my parents remained farm laborers. They had sired five girls and five boys. We seemed like two distinct families. The first six children had been born about one year apart. After the sixth child's birth, however, it was six years before my twin, and I were born. Two years after our births, Karen was born. Three years later my mother gave birth to what would be her tenth and final child. My sister Frances was born. Frances was the baby and she knew it. She was not spoiled, but she had nine protectors. We wanted to make sure her life was easier than ours. I wish I could say we were successful. In fact, I now know we were not.

Momma's primary motivation in family matters was to maintain harmony in our home. She tried to keep us together. Although she had not experienced any formal schooling, when the older brothers and sisters were going to elementary school, grades one to four, she insisted they teach her their assignments as they learned them. Whenever possible, she completed their homework with them. This continued until the assignments surpassed her capacity to understand or their capability to teach. It is also possible that Father forced her to stop. In any event, she was no longer illiterate, but her education was equal to that of a smart fourth grader.

Small children and the uneducated don't realize the limitations of inadequate education when it is happening to them. Momma always seemed wise to me. She was smart, though she had not been given the opportunity of being taught by professional teachers. At first glance Momma didn't appear to be much different from any of the other mothers living in our neighborhood. Yet many of them relied on her. They valued her advice. I remember many different occasions when she would be helping these women learn to read or teaching them to correctly add bills that had to be paid. She would help them reconcile grocery receipts from the owner of the local food market so that they would know how much they could spend before the end of the month when their bill would come due. She would help them correctly add timesheets of hours worked so that they could be sure the field contractor paid them the correct amount for that week's work.

Momma felt bad when her weakening health prevented her from spending time helping others. She began to realize that she was seriously ill. Starting this year, her heart trouble had become a part of our daily lives. Each year it got worse. I will never forget a day when I arrived home from school, the street was full of police cars, fire trucks, and an ambulance. Red and blue lights were flashing. Different pitched sirens could be heard.

At first, I thought the drama was taking place at our next-door neighbor's home. She was quite old, and, had not been well. As I approached closer to our home, I was met by a policeman who told us to "run along" because someone in the house was really sick and would be coming out of the house any minute, and access to the ambulance needed to be free of any bystanders. I looked again at the exact house where all of the commotion was taking place. It was our house and now I was experiencing alarm I had not felt before or since.

I screamed, "That is my house. What is happening? What is wrong?" The policeman offered his extended hand toward me as he bent down to be at a closer level to me. "Is Mrs. Reel your mom?" he asked.

I had tears running down my checks and my nose was running. I could only muster short sobbing words, "Yes, that is my Momma. Can I see her?" I had no more gotten those words out when I noticed one of the firemen was bringing her out on a stretcher. Another was running interference, getting people to move out of the way. The other two were pushing her toward the ambulance.

One of our neighbors, who lived across the street had made her way to where I was standing. "Officer, let me take care of this baby and his brother, when I find him, for Mrs Reel, until their Daddy or one of the married kids gets here." She took hold of my hand and pulled me to her side and smothered me into her apron patting my back and playing with the top of my hair as she said, "Everything is gonna be fine baby cause God gonna work it out. Come on now and let's get some chocolate cookies." I could not accept or express the fact that my mother might die at any moment. In fact, I was not even sure what that meant. Soon I began hearing others talk about how she might not make it next time. Not one person said when that time might happen. So, I started paying attention each day for signs of her having a heart attack.

When our older siblings would visit us after this incident, they tried to prepare us for the possible outcome of Momma's heart condition by noting that she was becoming more and more reliant on her nitroglycerin pills. We were told to make sure we knew at all times where her nitroglycerin medication was located. We soon learned that her dresser served as the medicine cabinet that contained the miracle drug that kept Momma alive. We were reminded that if Momma needed her medication and she didn't get it right away, she would probably die. As I look back now, that was a lot of pressure to put on young children.

The doctor had told Momma she should not continue working in the fields. He had informed her she was not to exert herself physically. Momma had replied that until the doctor could help us pay our bills, she had to work. She always carried her nitroglycerin pills with her when she worked in the fields. She said she could tell right before she would black out, and she would stop what she was doing long enough for the medication to take effect and the pain to become bearable.

I knew she lived in constant pain. I hoped that one day I could afford to pay for her medical bills and whatever else she needed. If I could earn enough to resolve the financial issues confronting us, she would not have to work. For myself, I knew I could escape the cycle of poverty we were in, if I could work and educate myself. I hoped my mother would stay alive until that time arrived.

Most people at this time felt the male should be the leader of the family unit. That role was usually held by the father. In the case of our family, however, the leadership role was assumed by Momma. I had to look elsewhere for a strong father image to emulate because something blocked the normal relationship that could and should have existed between Father and me.

I guess it really doesn't matter whether it was Father's limited exposure to assertive boys, or my unwillingness to pretend to like farm work. The fact existed that we had few feelings for one another. Father never displayed any real affection toward me. My twin and I had been placed in a difficult position. Because there were two of us, and two parents, we had been parceled out. I had been given to Momma to help with the everyday household chores. Donald had been given to Father to help with all outdoor jobs. I had been left out of my father's life, while my twin worked closely with him.

I found an answer to my yearning to be closer to my father at the God's Holy Assembly Church I attended. The pastor took the place of a father image in my life. I have no doubt that I would have never made it through my teen years had it not been for the members of my church and the constant caring of the pastor. Pastor Robert DeWolfe, our minister, became the person who gave me the will to succeed. I wanted so very much to please him. I wanted to grow up and be just like him. He had a son, Larry, four years older than I, and I noticed immediately how much the two of them loved and respected each other.

I spent much time learning from both. I wanted to have a relationship like they had.

I began attending the church faithfully when I was twelve years old and in sixth grade. My first visit had been truly serendipitous. My parents were driving me to see the doctor on a hot summer Wednesday, when I noticed a sign placed in front of a church, which was only a few blocks from our home. The sign advertised an evening service that night during Vacation Bible School. It was called a "Healing Service."

We were headed to the doctor's office because I was experiencing an extremely high level of pain that particular morning. I felt extremely uncomfortable and my entire body ached. I knew something very extraordinary was happening inside of me. My body was experiencing extreme pain in both my legs and both my arms. Muscle spasms were quick and sharp; they happened irregularly. My muscles would tighten up and I would spring forward to a sitting position. Rheumatic fever was claiming another victim. This extreme pain had started the night before; however, it had gotten better during the middle of the night; only to come back after I woke up earlier that morning. In fact, it was worse at that time than it had been the night before. I remembered the previous night when Momma tried her best to help me.

She sat on the side of the bed trying to comfort me. She was Cherokee Indian, and her beautiful black hair and high cheekbones verified her ancestry. I always thought she was a beautiful woman. She loved telling stories of her childhood and how she had played on the Indian reservation. She often talked about learning how to dance and how to be creative. She was very talented when it came to making things with her hands. She taught us how to use our imaginations to explore places we had not experienced firsthand.

Momma spent the night singing and telling stories about her childhood in order to try and comfort me. This type of comforting was second nature to her. Suddenly, however, she became silent, frozen, rigid. I thought she was preparing to act out one of the special songs she had, using hand and facial gestures to depict what was transpiring in the song. She would use this type of ancient mime for interpretation purposes. She lifted my hand and placed it around her. Then I thought we were about to play some type of game. Since I had been bedridden for some time with my first battle of rheumatic fever, I welcomed the tender love and care being offered by Momma.

"Ron, I'm sorry to have to ask you to do this, but I am having trouble breathing and I need your help. Will you slip your hand up and unfasten my bra strap?" she asked. Her voice was strained and very weak.

I hesitated for just a second. Momma was asking me to help her. I had been ill many times in my life. When I was ten, I had suffered from my first bout with rheumatic fever. What none of my family members knew or understood was that this disease develops as a complication from inadequately treated strep throat caused by an infection from the streptococcus bacteria. I thought they said I had "romantic fever." I used my imagination to come up with an interpretation I could understand; none of the adults chose to explain the disease to me. My older brothers and sisters were always kissing their mates. It was not long after I saw them kissing each other that they would announce they were going to have a baby. Therefore, I concluded if I had romantic fever and kissed any girl, we would soon have a baby also!

This second time I battled with rheumatic fever; I had not been able to do anything physical for myself for almost three months. Only a few hours earlier, I had been carried from my bed to the bathroom. The doctors had forbidden me from getting up from my bed to go the few steps to our one bathroom. I had a heart murmur and irregular heart beating when I tried any type of physical activity, even walking.

Now Momma had asked me to help her. Of course, I would obey. Once I unsnapped the hooks, I felt Momma sigh with obvious relief.

"Now, will you go over and take one of my nitroglycerin pills out of the bottle on the dresser and put it underneath my tongue?" she asked. I once again did as she requested. Momma's eyes looked deep and dark. There now appeared a glaze of helplessness. Her shallow breathing began to change to deeper breaths. I could see her taking in more air and I could feel the exhaled air hitting my face. Slowly the mother I knew was returning. After a few minutes the twinkle in her eyes returned.

"Son, I haven't ever asked any of you kids to do anything like that for me. I hope you will forgive me for having to ask you for help," she said.

"Momma, it's okay. I would do anything I can for you," I replied. Suddenly, she realized I was up and out of bed. I had not left my bed for the past three months under my own power. I had to be carried from my bed to the living room, to the table to eat with the family, and as I already shared with you, to the bathroom when that time was appropriate.

"Now you better get back in bed yourself before you get too tired," she said. She tucked my covers around me and kissed me on the forehead.

Momma always put her concern about her children, her husband, and others before herself. Momma was a large woman. Her appearance had been hardened slightly by the years of stooping in the agricultural fields. Her hands were rough but loving. Her outward appearance would suggest a calloused woman. Many of the women who worked in the fields, had many children, few conveniences, and no extra money to spend on themselves; some of them looked less feminine than women with the ability to spend money on their own needs.

With my mother taken care of, my thoughts returned to my own condition. My head seemed like it was about to explode. My left ear drum popped. My temperature, I learned later, reached 104 degrees; but I felt very cold. Momma tried to make me warm by placing more blankets over me.

Our house seemed quite breezy because of the holes in the walls where the sheetrock was supposed to, but did not, meet the foundation. These holes allowed outside air to enter the house at will. The children's bedroom was beside my parent's room. We had two large double beds set up at both ends of the room with a wire and curtains separating the room into the boys' side and the girls' side. My bed was next to the door that went into my parents' bedroom. Their room did not have any sheetrock covering the bare foundation studs.

As I lay there shivering, I thought I would die soon. In fact, a doctor had told my parents that I had only six months to live. All I knew for sure was that I felt miserable. I tried not to cry. With all my might, I tried not to cry. The tears, however, came uncontrollably. Momma was sitting there beside me doing her best to comfort me. Even though she was next to me, I was still afraid.

She began to wash my face with a washcloth soaked in ice water. Occasionally, she would let the washcloth slip down and touch my chest, my stomach, even my legs. Then she would bring the wet cloth back up my body. It was cold, but it felt good. It brought a nice soothing and refreshing tingle to my body. It reminded me of the hot days of summer when we children were allowed to spray each other with the water hose. That first burst of cold water was always so refreshing; yet, so absolutely startling to the body.

Momma turned out the lamp. The room became dark. When I looked at Momma, she appeared to have a halo around her. I thought it was because she had angelic qualities. My eyes soon adjusted to the dark and the halo disappeared.

As I looked at Momma, she appeared very tired. I knew she had worked all day in the fields pulling, hacking, shoveling, and beating weeds from the ground. It didn't seem to bother her that she would soon be forced to return to the fields. The only important concern of the moment was her son's welfare.

"Momma, am I going to die?" I asked. She didn't respond. Her eyes met mine for just a second. They didn't appear perplexed nor were they skittish. She was the kind of person who would never lie to you, but she did not answer.

"Please hold my hand, Momma," I requested. "I am scared, and I don't want to die. If you hold my hand, I won't be scared," I whispered. With all of the tender love that only a mother can give a small child, she took hold of my hand gently but firmly. I felt at ease and experienced a peace that I had rarely felt. The aching and throbbing of my legs, arms, and back began to subside. It was like the pain was being forced to leave my body.

For what seemed like a half hour, she did not speak. I decided to hold my breath to see if I could force her to say something because she would see that I was not breathing. Finally, her mouth opened, and her lips formed loving words of gentle explanation. She licked her lips, took a deep long and sustained breath of air, gently exhaled, and with her tongue she moistened her lips and began:

"Ronald, God puts each of us in this world for a special reason. We don't always know that reason right away. In fact, sometimes we don't know until much later in life, if we discover it at all. Some of us are born to live long lives. Some only have a short life here on this earth. Some people, like the rich, live life having all the money they need so they can buy material things like the best medical care that's available. Some of us live without much money. We cannot buy certain things because we cannot pay for them. But we have other things that are just for us. We have things that money cannot buy. You cannot buy love. Love must be earned. You earn love by doing good deeds for other people when they need help. You don't do things for them cause you think you will get something for it. You do it cause it is the right thing to do and they have either asked for help or you know they need your help."

"Each person born is like a reflection in a mirror for other people. If you look and study someone, you can find things you like as well as things you dislike. You can find some qualities in other people just like in yourself. Some of those qualities are good, some are bad, some are strong, and some are weak. We all have similar qualities; that is what makes us able to get along. We are not all exactly alike, but enough alike to call us friends or family. Each of us affects those around us. God has us all here for His chosen amount of time. None of knows when we are gonna die. Only God knows for sure. If it is your time, God will take you. If it is not your time, our prayers for what is best in your life, and the healing that we all want for you will come true."

"But Momma, the doctor said I only had six months to live; and it has been three months since he told us that in his office," I reminded her. Tears were now streaming down my cheeks. My heart was beating fast. I did not want to die. I did not want to leave my twin, my sisters, Momma, or even Father. I could not understand what dying meant. I had so many questions! I asked some of them: "What will happen to me? Will I be able to fly to heaven? Will I even go to heaven? What if I have not been good enough and don't make it to heaven? Exactly where am I going to go when I die? Do I just go to sleep and don't wake up? Will I be able to see my family, but they not be able to see me? Will I be by myself? Will I get any older? Will there be a school where I end up after dying? Will anyone know me at the place where I am about to go?"

I had so many questions, but Momma made no attempt to answer them. I reached out to be embraced by someone I felt could cure me. She gathered me like a big rag doll in her strong caring arms. "Son, you are not gonna help matters by crying. We have prayed. We have to leave all the rest up to someone greater than us. I believe in Him and His will. While I have not always lived the life, He wants us to live, you have lived as He instructed us to live. You are kind and caring. You share with others. You are polite. You help with chores when you see something needs to be done. You do your homework and help your brother and sisters with their work. You put other peoples' needs as a priority. He will have His way. You have to be brave and strong. You must learn to trust. We all have to trust each other. We also have to trust Him," she concluded.

I did trust Momma. I knew she would not do anything that would harm me. I wanted to get better so I could repay her kindness and love that she so expertly administered every single day. I suddenly felt like I wanted to sleep. Peace and tranquility began to return to my body. It was as though the rheumatic fever was being slowly driven from my body. My strength was being restored. I could sleep only because I felt Momma and God were there with me that night.

At least that is how I remember it. As I wrote earlier, on Wednesday morning as we headed toward the doctor's office, I saw the church sign about the healing service. As we drove by the church and I saw the banner, I wanted to know if I could attend? I was quickly and emphatically told by Momma that I was not strong enough to attend that service. That was not enough to stop me. I snuck out of the house that evening and somehow walked the few blocks to the church. As I sat in the back of the church during the service, I saw a number of individuals speak out in agreement when the speaker would say things about the great power that was given these people through Jesus. Toward the end of the service some people around me were standing and speaking in languages I could not understand. It was a bit frightening, but also at the same time, it was exciting.

I also remember the evangelist asking if there was someone in the audience who had a heart problem. He was looking in my direction. I thought he was looking directly at me. I made my way down to the front of the church. As I approached him, he raised his hands and then placed them on my head and then on my shoulders. At the very moment he placed his hands on me, I felt a cleansing rush through my body. I felt energetic and heard him telling me to claim the healing out loud. I spoke, "I am healed. Heart murmur be gone." He and the people around me began to sing praises about how powerful and mighty God was in the past, is currently, and will be in the future.

I went home with a secret that I did not reveal until my next visit to the doctor. My next scheduled doctor visit was one week from that day. I knew I was changed, energetic, cured. For the next week I was constantly being caught performing daily chores that had been forbidden by the doctor. I got so tired of being told to stop doing these tasks, I stopped doing them until the big reveal. As we approached the doctor's office, I informed Momma that today the doctor was going to say I could go back to school and that I was no longer sick. My mother had been with me in the past when I would temporarily get better only to get worse overnight. This time it was different. The doctor first told us he did not hear any heart murmur, my coloring was good, and my blood pressure was normal. His words described it best when he said, "I don't necessarily believe in God, but I have no explanation for what has transpired in Ronald's body."

I knew. I asked if I could return to school. He made a deal with me. He ran some additional blood tests and ask for me to wait the two days it would take to get the results back from the laboratory. Two days later I was able to return to school.

Mr. Tanner, my teacher, had been providing home schooling to me while I was bedridden. He had come three days a week at 3:30 p.m. so I would not get behind in my schooling. I thought this one-on-one teaching was wonderful. He seemed amazed at how well I was doing in my studies. I had nothing to do each day except to do my homework. Every week he would bring assignments, materials, books, articles, and handouts he had created to facilitate an advanced curriculum designed specifically for me. He seemed shocked when I walked into class. His smile and stance made me glow with glee and joy. I couldn't tell who was happier for me to be back in school. He made me feel wanted.

It happened that on the day I returned, report cards were being given to the students to take home and have parents sign and return. Some of the students seemed shocked when Mr. Tanner called my name and handed me a report card. Janet Goats said, "He hasn't been here for months. How can he receive a report card?" Before Mr. Tanner could respond, Anthony Costello loudly called from the back of the room, "It's probably all F's because he's missed everything." Some of the other class members began to chuckle. Mr. Tanner seized on a very teachable moment. "Class settle down. I think we all should welcome Ron back to school. He has been very sick. He is now fully recovered from his illness and I know you all want to join me in welcoming him back. The school has a special program to help students with their studies when they are ill. It is an after-school study program where the school district sends teachers out to the home of a student who is too ill to attend school for an extended period of time. I personally have been teaching Ron for the past several months three times a week. He is not behind in any of his subjects. In fact, he is ahead in a couple of subjects. He actually has earned straight A's!"

My friend Tommy jumped up from his seat and started applauding. Soon almost the entire class was cheering. I don't know if it was just a reaction that takes place in a moment of exhilaration, or if most of the students were truly happy, I was back. What I do know, is that I was very proud and felt I wanted to someday be a teacher like him so I could help students like me learn and prosper. I thought Mr. Tanner saw something so special in me that he was willing to make sure my journey out of the fields would take place. I thought he saw a quality in me that I had not seen in myself at that age. I was so grateful my teacher had volunteered to come to my house after he completed his regular day of work.

He had not come just for me. He had come because of me. Teachers, real teachers, teach for the love of sharing information to children so they can make intelligent and reasoned decisions. I know in my heart; Mr. Tanner will always be a role model for me to emulate.

We moved from Selma to Fowler two months into my eighth-grade year. By this time one of my favorite classes was PE. I had never liked PE much because of my constant battling with illnesses during earlier grades. Since my "healing," I was able to breathe better and could suddenly run without being in pain and found myself faster than most of the other children. The teacher informed us that for the next six weeks we were going to learn how to do western dancing. We were separated into groups of eight; four boys and four girls. I enjoyed the steps and staging of this type of dancing. It was not as fast nor as stiff as I had thought it would be. Besides, we got to hold hands with the girls.

I had never held hands with any girls besides my sisters before. One girl immediately caught my eye. She was especially pretty, and she smiled at me when we would be paired as partners. Her name was Susan Manson. Her parents owned a cattle farm and ranch right outside of Fowler. When the bus would take us home after school, it took about five minutes to drive down the road to get to her house, one of the largest in the area. About the second week of riding the bus, I found Susan sitting either behind or in front of where I would sit. One day I started a conversation concerning an assignment for our PE class. We had just learned that at the end of the semester, we were to display our dancing as a part of a western celebration held within the community.

Soon, Susan and I were sitting together in the same seat, almost oblivious to the other bus riders. During one of our conversations, Susan suggested that we might go to a movie together sometime. I did not really think much of it because I had only been to one movie my entire life and that was one Saturday evening when Momma and Father went to a dance and they took the four of us kids to the movie which was located next to where they were going to be dancing. They wanted some free time away from us. We got to see "Swiss Family Robinson." The place where they were going was next to the theater. It was a bar, but Momma called it a dance studio.

When riding the bus to and from school, Susan and I would, from time to time, brush up against each other; have our arms touch, even have our fingers barely touch without actually holding hands. I did not know what these new feelings were that I was experiencing. I found them exciting, but at the same time I did not know how I was supposed to respond. I did not know if Susan was experiencing similar feelings and I did not have the courage to ask her. I enjoyed being with her. I liked our discussions, which ranged from school gossip, to current events, style and fashion.

I wanted to find out how I should proceed with exploring what I thought might be a boyfriend-girlfriend relationship. I knew two people I thought would be able to help me understand what I was experiencing. I decided to talk with both Momma and then with Father. I first approached Momma. "I was wondering if I could talk to you about something that I am confused about and need some expert advice from someone that could help me?" I asked in a very unsure manner.

"You do know you can ask me anything?" Momma responded.

"I have met this girl at school named Susan and I think I like her. I have never felt like this before."

"What do you like about this girl?" Momma asked.

"I like the way she smiles; her eyes are beautiful, she is pretty; we talk about everything; and we never fight," I revealed.

"Well, at about this age, boys and girls begin the process of adulthood. Your body is searching for a special person that completes you. Your body is going through what some adults call "hormone changes." You are leaving the child phase of your life and beginning the adult phase. You will have many friends who are girls; but a special connection that causes every fiber in your body to tingle, that causes you to light up with joy when she walks into a room or arrives at a place after you have been separated; that causes you to think positive thoughts about that person day and night; and when all of these things happen, it is God's way of letting you know you are special and not meant to be alone. Am I making this any clearer?" she asked.

"I think so," I replied.

"Do you have the same reactions and feelings when you are around other girls?" Momma asked.

"No! I want those other girls to like me, but I don't feel they need me or excite me in a way Susan does," I replied.

"God wants us to be wanted, loved, and cared for in a special way. These feelings eventually arrive at the ultimate level of expression when two people have sex and explore the ultimate joy of pleasing each other. You both will make each other complete by touching, kissing, and reacting to the needs of the other, resulting in making the other person first and you second, causing you to feel wonderful in a way that no words can adequately express.

But having sex should be experienced only when you are married. The urge may be there, but you must exercise control over it until after you marry. Ask yourself if you are ready to commit to this one person? The Bible teaches it is when a man and a woman decide to marry each other in a public ceremony, showing all their friends and family they have decided to be together legally. That public display and the ring one wears shows anyone looking, you are committed to only one person. There will be nothing in your life more fulfilling than having sex with the person you love. It has to be something both of you want and are ready to do with each other," she explained. I suddenly had many questions to ask, "How will I know when the time is right? How will I know what to do? How do I get trained? How far do I go with a girl?"

She replied, "All of these things will be answered as you progress through life. I am sure your health class will give you answers to what to do part. Before marriage, if at any point she tells you to stop or feels uncomfortable, you stop. When she tells you to stop, that does not mean she won't ever want to continue; but at that moment in time, she is not ready and if you are not married you should not be doing it in the first place. If you love her, you will honor her by stopping no matter how difficult it might be. To continue would be putting your needs before hers. I think that is enough on this subject for today. We can talk about this when you have further questions," Momma completed her little talk, reached over, took my hands, and smiled. She had another thought, "You are growing up. Treat every person you have feelings for the way you want to be treated and you won't go wrong."

I told Momma I thought I should ask Father for his view. Momma told me she did not think that would be a good idea.

"I am afraid your Father will tell you to only think of yourself. He might leave out the part of being married also! God will always love us. He loves us more when we obey his commandments. Having sex before marriage is breaking one of those commandments. You must always think of what you do in light of how it meets the needs of the other person, and if you are married that will be an easier decision" she said.

She told me if I had unanswered questions after a couple of days to return and she would be more than happy to clarify any questions. I decided there was no need to seek any clarification from Father. It seemed simple to me; I would always follow Momma's advice.

Susan and I went to the movies the next weekend. I will never forget that evening. We sat side by side. I could feel the electricity. I looked at her and she made me happy. Our hands touched and an excitement of tenderness that only touch can bring aroused a feeling deep within my entire body. We held hands. By the end of the evening, we shared our first kiss. It lasted about one second in real time, but it felt like fireworks were going off all around us. We went on several more dates. We had more holding of hands, kissing, and a little touching; but neither of us were ready for sex any time soon.

I realized from this first relationship, I would never take advantage of anyone and that my duty was, is, and always will be to make sure the needs of the other person are treated as important or even more important than mine. The word "No" means just that. The word "Stop" means just that! If your partner doesn't want to continue, that means you don't continue. No part of love is greater than making sure that the needs of the other person are being met. If you love them that much, you are one lucky person. That is fulfillment. That is love.

In some ways our family had been very fortunate. Although Father and Momma each made about $60.00 per month as farm laborers, Father would take side jobs fixing things for people to earn extra money for us. Father saw to it we never went very hungry, without clothes to wear, or without a place to call home. Sometimes we had to eat bread and gravy three times a day; yet we never went to bed without having eaten.

The fact that many of our clothes were hand-me-downs did not matter to us. After Momma altered them, they always fit, and she made sure they were clean. Our home differed from town to town. Once we had to live in two small farmhouses; another time in a house that had only a dirt floor, which we cleaned and swept every day. Besides, a family exists outside of the restraints of material items. A house is a building. A home is a family full of human beings sometimes related by blood; sometimes related by love; residing together in a dwelling.

Through the trials and tribulations of poverty, we never once felt bad because we lacked money. We children were not aware of the financial problems facing our parents. We seemed to have everything we needed. I took it for granted that water was always available if you were dirty and needed a bath or were thirsty and needed a drink. I thought the lights automatically turned on if you pushed or turned on the switch. I thought you got into your car, started it, and drove it to the place you wanted to go. I did not think that you might not be able to drive anywhere if you could not afford to purchase gasoline from the one station in town that sold it. I just thought there was some reason my parents did not want to go to a location we asked to visit. It did not dawn on me that their lack of attendance at school events, for example, may have been due to the fact, that what little gasoline they could afford was reserved for driving to work and not for social events.

With the exception of my eighth-grade graduation, neither of my parents ever attended my school functions, church activities, or social events. All the other kids had at least one, but usually both, of their parents in attendance; but I was always picked up and returned home by a friend's parent, an adult from church, a teacher, or a mentor.

Occasionally, we would drive to Uncle Bill's or Aunt Dovie's. Today such a visit would be considered a "staycation," but that word was not in use when we were doing it. As I look back now at moments from my childhood, it is hard to believe that I thought most utilities came with the house, but I did. It was not until I was in middle school or later that I realized that water, phone service, and gas for cooking had to be paid for separately. I realized this when my parents were late with a payment and one or more of these utilities stopped working. When that happened, Momma would blush and explain that the electricity or gas owned and operated by Pacific Gas and Electric had been turned off because we could not afford to pay the bill on time. At first, this did not bother me. Anytime there was no water, electricity, or phone service for a couple of days Momma treated it as an adventure. It was fun to play tag in the dark or pretend to make phone calls to our friends and relatives.

At the same time, she tried to teach us a life lesson from these "little setbacks" as she called them. She wanted us to learn to accept responsibility for helping out in the home even when it had to be done in the dark. What I learned was that those items like electricity, water, and gas were luxuries that could be provided for us because our parents were working and thus able to pay for them. Once I got out on my own and had to come up with money for these items each month, I realized how lucky I was as a child to have parents who could afford them, even if there were a few interruptions or "setbacks."

Another thing I learned about this time was that I did not want to continue living the same day-to-day kind of existence my parents lived. Our family never planned a trip to Disneyland, never went to the coast on a vacation, never ate in a restaurant that offered waiter service. We would never go to the doctor before we had an emergency. We did not seek dental care unless it was to have a tooth extracted. We did not join any clubs or play sports that cost money to participate.

Momma hid all the stress that comes with poverty as much as humanly possible. On the night Momma suffered her second major heart attack and I was the only one home with her at the time, I realized that she was the one responsible for keeping our family together. After I got her nitroglycerin pills for her, she told me how special she thought I was. She predicted I would be the one to climb out of the impoverished condition in which we lived. She was sure this lifestyle was only a temporary stop for me, but I was to never forget where I came from because it taught me character and love. I did not know how I would climb out of poverty; only that I would.

Through all the years of struggle, one member of the family was generally silent. He told us little about himself or about his feelings, but when he did, he was loud and clear. Father worked long hours seven days a week. I always thought it strange when kids talked about their fathers going places with them, sharing, or helping them do things because our father was rarely home. He was at work before we got up in the morning and he often did not return until it was almost bedtime. Father was illiterate. He had never been taught how to read or write. Until the day he died, he always signed his name with a big X.

He was, however, mechanically inclined and street smart. Momma claimed many times while we were growing up, that had Father been given the opportunity for education, he would have been a financial success story. I am not so sure of this. I am sure he was a strict disciplinarian.

After working in the fields for twelve to sixteen hours, Father expected us to be silent when he arrived home. Children find it hard to believe that adults would retire for bed as early as 7:30 p.m.; but he did, saying, "To bed with the chickens; up with the chickens." Since we were seldom up at 4:30 a.m. when he went to work, we never had breakfast with him nor told him our plans for the day. We always thought Father was grumpy, but Momma defended him religiously. She would tell us of their courting days. She loved to remember how he was a "gentleman" when he came calling on her on the Indian reservation. She bragged that the other girls were jealous because he had selected her.

Momma always tried to justify Father's firm way of disciplining us. When we thought he was being too rough on us, she would tell us this story:

"When your father was a little boy, his daddy was not very kind to him. His older brother was more like a father. His brother helped him learn to hunt so he would not starve. He taught him to cook, iron, and fix things so he could provide for himself. Your grandpa used to try to embarrass your father. He would send him to a corner of the house where he was made to stand on his tiptoes. Your grandpa would then draw a round circle on the corner of the wall and then put your dad's nose in that circle. While your dad was standing on his tiptoes, grandpa would hit him with a strap, or rope, or a branch from a tree. If your dad screamed out or took his nose out of the circle, he would get hit again! Your dad could not cry; if he did, he was beaten again because Grandpa Reel did not think men should cry."

That story lost the power it held for me the first few times I heard it, when I saw Father use that same disciplinary tactic on us. He only knew what he had been taught by his father. Because he was not educated and had never been exposed to other disciplinary techniques, he did to us what had been done to him.

Momma wanted us to see Father as a victim. She claimed that although he had survived a horrible childhood, he chose to have a family of his own so he could give his children a better life than he had experienced. She hoped that if we saw Father as a victim instead of the perpetrator, we might forgive him for his lack of parenting skills.

We listened to her and tried to understand his behavior, but we thought he was never going to adopt a more humane way to discipline his children, a way that did not rely on using a belt, rope, or tree branch. We were correct; he never did. Discipline came often. None of us would ever forget what it was like to be punished by Father. His form of discipline stopped only when he tired from the hard spanking, he was administering to us.

My twin viewed school somewhat like we saw Father's discipline. He hated it; and somehow, he managed to avoid it when it came to homework assigned to him. I loved school. My parents could not understand why Donald never had any homework, and I always had tons of it. He had homework; he just never did it.

Because of Father's lights out at 9:00 p.m. policy, I often had to study at night underneath my covers with a flashlight. Father never could understand why his flashlight battery was so ineffective. If homework was not finished before the lights were turned out, it had to be finished in the morning after the sun was up. "If you can pay the electric bill, you can stay up later," he promised. I did all my homework. I studied hard, had good grades, and planned to attend college so I would not have to continue the kind of life we were living in Clovis.

All of my immediate family members had stayed within a twenty-mile radius after leaving home. I do not remember Father ever considering a move away from Fresno County. I do not remember Father ever complaining about work, the heat, the cold, nor even all of us kids until Momma became so ill. I think many members of my family, including Father, did not leave the area because they were afraid, they could not find anything better.

One time, Father's boss gave him written instructions on how to reach a farm in Kerman, a small town about thirty miles away, where he was needed to fix some farm equipment. Father pretended he could read the instructions, but as soon as his boss left, Father called me over to help him. He asked me to explain to him how to get there using specific houses and businesses at certain corners as a road map for him to follow.

I did as he requested, using landmarks he knew to guide him to the farm; he found it. Father may have needed help with written driving instruction to places he had never been before, but he never asked anyone for help when it came to mechanical issues. If some equipment broke down, he could figure out a way to fix it. Father did not share his feelings, desires, wants, or needs with anyone. Even today, for example, I have no idea why he did not at least try to learn how to read, as Momma had done. He kept his secrets hidden from all.

CHAPTER FOUR

Moving from one location to the next and then back again was part of my life. During my freshman year in high school, we moved from Fowler back to Clovis. My counselor enrolled me in an introduction to acting course. Within the first week, I felt this class would be fun and worthwhile in helping me understand how different people could express emotions such as humor, resentment, tragedy, and fantasy. When I enrolled in the class, Mr. Mason was teaching a section about children's theatre. This year he was going to direct the play "The Wizard of Oz" for our school's fall production. He was trying to recruit stage crew and extra people who could help him with the props, the painting of sets, publicity, and ticket sales. He wanted those of us in this freshman class to help with the production, but not to act in it because he already had a number of experienced upperclassmen who could do that. He told us he was having an open audition for all character roles after school if any of us wanted to drop by and see what an audition was like.

I went to the audition where I found myself sitting right in the midst of excitement and controlled chaos. Mr. Mason was sitting in the middle of the auditorium (the orchestra area) and other students were seated around him. He would call them up to the stage to read from various scenes. When Mr. Mason noticed me at the corner of the stage, he motioned for me to come and sit in the area where all of the other students were sitting. He made the following announcement:

"This year the Fresno County School District is sponsoring a new competition where a set of seven judges are going to come to each of the schools' fall productions and choose five shows to be invited to perform a showcase in the two thousand seat auditorium at Fresno High School during the last week of the fall term. No children's show has ever been chosen. I want that to change. So, you junior and senior students, we must be better than we have been in the past. I need you to commit to doing your best work. Can I count on you?"

This news was greeted with a surge of applause and shouts of agreement from most of the students. To a freshman many of these students look so much older. It is amazing how much physical growth takes place in just three to four years. As the various students would leave their seats and go to the stage, their friends in the audience would shout out their names, say encouraging words, and whistle. I had never seen such support being given between students before.

At one point during the tryouts, Mr. Mason told everyone to take a break. It was during this time I discovered that most of the students auditioning were seniors who had been acting for three or more years. Several were juniors who had earned special recognition from Mr. Mason for the work they had done the previous year. None were freshmen.

Mr. Mason looked at me and asked, "Ron, why are you here? Want to learn from our best, or are you here to see how you can help?"

"I didn't have anything else to do today so I thought I would come and see how this auditioning works."

"This is our highest-level production. These students have shown dedication and ability previously. We do a couple of in-class productions that are open to any student taking a drama class, but this production is going to fill the house and take us to the showcase," he predicted.

"Can anyone audition?" I asked.

"Technically yes! But this audition is pretty much by invitation only."

"Who extends the invitation?"

"I do. You want one?"

"I like the story. I went and read both the play and the book. This story shows care, understanding, and conflict on all different emotional levels. In a number of ways, I really identify with the Cowardly Lion."

"Stick around, and if we have some time at the end of tonight's rehearsal, I may have to ask you to read," he jested. After he said that to me, I could tell that he had upset some of the older students who were close enough to hear us. I heard one male student say to another, "No freshman will ever be part of this cast."

The audition continued. To a novice judge like me, they all read their parts very well. I did not know who he was going to pick for the roles. Finally, Mr.

Mason turned to me and asked, "You want to read for me?"

I responded quickly, "Sure."

"Take a script from one of the guys and turn to page ten," he commanded. At first no guy offered a script. In fact, most of the guys held their scripts down to their sides and began to walk away.

"Someone, give Ron your script!" The senior that had been reading for the Cowardly Lion responded to this suggestion quickly, "Oh, I am sorry Mr. Mason, I didn't hear you." He walked over and slammed the folded script down on the chair next to me as hard as he could.

"I need a girl to read Dorothy with Ron!"

Mr. Mason motioned for one of the girls to take the stage with me. She was one of the juniors who had earned special recognition and honors last year. When she had been on stage earlier, I had heard some of the senior girls talking about how good she was; but they thought Mr. Mason would go with only seniors in all major roles this year. I heard some of the other students talking about who they thought would win the main roles.

She and I read together the portion of the script he had requested. He then asked us to go to one of the last scenes in the play. We read again for him. Suddenly when we finished, he thanked us and announced that in five minutes he would be posting the names of the people he wanted to "call back" the next day for further readings. He retreated to his office. All of the students were congratulating each other on how well they all had done. It appeared to me some of the statements were sincere, but some of the students were not encouraging with their comments.

Mr. Mason returned and posted his list. Before he posted, however, he said to the entire group, "Some of you will be surprised. I want you to know this was the best audition I have had since taking over the drama program. You are all to be congratulated. I will give everyone who has auditioned for one of these roles a part in the show."

The students gathered around the list he taped on the stage door. Everyone was surprised that my name was posted. A couple of the senior boys pushed their way past me. They did not smile nor speak. The junior girl who had read with me was the first to come up and congratulate me.

The next day I arrived about twenty minutes early. The auditorium was open, but I did not find anyone on stage or in the "house" as it is called. I decided to go up to the balcony so I could see what audience members saw from high up above the stage. While I was up there, three of girls arrived on stage. I am sure they assumed they were alone.

The brunette asked, "Who is this Ron guy? Does anyone know him? His clothes don't look like they came from Macy's; more like hand-me-downs if you ask me." The Redhead with short hair laughed at this statement. She reported, "He used to live out on Park Lane where all the Okies live. I think they have about 15 people living in a one-bedroom house. He goes to that small church the Anderson family runs. None of them out there have much going for them."

The blonde girl who had read with me spoke up, "I thought he was nice. He is really a good actor too."

The brunette responded, "It's not fair. People have to pay their dues. Seniors and then juniors should get the parts not freshmen."

The redhead with the short hair kept the conversation going, "It's not that I have anything against him personally. I don't know him. I don't socialize with freshmen. I just don't like his kind. They always feel like things should be given to them."

My heroine, the blonde, seemed shocked to hear this. "Where have the two of you been Sunday after Sunday when in church, we have been taught to be tolerant and accepting? None of us have the power to choose who is our family. Did you not learn anything from the sermons all these years?"

The redhead answered her, "I don't really have anything against him, but he is a freshman. He still looks like a junior high student. He hasn't worked for this opportunity. Besides, he may not even be here at the end of the term; those people always move around with the crops."

The blonde was quick to come to my defense, "We don't know that. We haven't been able to place in county competition ever. Perhaps what we need is new talent. Why argue, girls? He has not gotten the part yet."

By this time, Mr. Mason was on stage calling for all of those scheduled for the call back to assemble. I quietly came down to the main floor and exited one of the side doors. I went to the back of the auditorium and reentered so everyone thought I was just arriving.

Mr. Mason spent the next two hours pairing different people for various roles. It was during this time Mr. Mason informed us that once he cast us into a particular role, he would only address us by that character's name whether we were on stage, at school, or if he saw us in public. He wanted us to become and be recognized as that character. During the last half hour, he had the senior most of the cast wanted to win the role and me read for the Cowardly Lion and the blonde (a junior) and the brunette (a senior) read for Dorothy. All four of us got major roles. It was the first time in Clovis drama history that two of the starring roles were performed by a junior and a freshman.

After the district committee came and reviewed our production, another first in Clovis history occurred. We went to the showcase where we placed third. Neither Father nor Momma attended either of these award-winning performances.

A year later Dorothy as she was called while the play was running; and then I nicknamed her and called her Dot after the play and I would perform together again. This time it was October of my sophomore year, and I found myself experiencing more than just academics, running, drama, choir, church, and work; I decided to find a girlfriend. I saw many of my friends, both male and female, leave our circle and pair with another person. Doing this seemed to require a great deal of one-on-one energy and time but I was certainly willing to explore any possibility because part of me was feeling a void as my body was changing from boy to becoming a man.

I wanted someone who was bright so we could discuss serious topics. I wanted someone who enjoyed humor because so much of my life had been caught up in some form of drama. I longed for lightness and joyful moments in my life. I wanted someone who was accepting of people in general. I had already met people unwilling to see past financial status, race, or lack of athletic ability. It was, is, and will always be a part of my nature to accept people on the level where they are and grow together with them.

It appeared to me the junior and senior girls were more compatible with me and my goals than my freshmen and sophomore classmates. My freshman year and my social experiences with Dot during the "Wizard of Oz" play gave me someone worthy of consideration. We had made drama history by being the first junior and freshman leads in a major production. In the play I became her protector and I enjoyed feeling protective of her.

During rehearsals of the production, and even outside of school, we had a cordial relationship. She was always polite, and I knew she had defended me to her friends when it was needed. Now she was a senior and was extremely popular. Not only was she smart, but she was also very pretty. Her beauty was not just in her looks; she found positive qualities and good in all the people she met. I thought I had a crush on her, but I did not want anyone to know because of our age difference.

During my sophomore and her senior year, Dot faced a crisis. She was dating one of the star football players. He was running for Homecoming King and she was running for Homecoming Queen. The week before the football game and announcement of the winners, they broke up. One of her best friends, who was also my friend, told me Dot was devastated. She did not know what to do. Dot didn't want to go to the dance alone, but her other friends were already committed to going with someone else.

I sent word through our mutual friend I would be honored to accompany her if she needed someone. I sent her that message on Monday. On Tuesday I received a note back thanking me for being so considerate. Her note read, "I just don't know what to do." She did not comment on my willingness to be available as her escort.

On Wednesday our mutual friend told me she thought Dot would just go to Homecoming alone. Thursday morning Dot made it a point to see me before my first class started. She asked if we could meet after school. Dot showed up at the snack shack right at closing time. She wanted to go someplace to talk. She asked,

"Do you want to go with me to Dairy Delight for some fries and a coke?" This was the first time I had ever been asked out by a girl.

"How do we get there?" I responded.

"I have a license and a car. I can take us. Are you willing to ride with me?" It did not take long for me to answer. "But of course," I picked up my belongings, clocked out, and met Dot at the student parking lot. The Dairy Delight was only four blocks from the high school. Her parents had purchased her this new car at the beginning of the school year so she would be very familiar driving it when she went to UCLA as a freshman.

I went over to the driver's side of the car. I stood there waiting for her to unlock the car. "If you unlock the door, I will open your door for you," I explained.

"What? Nobody has ever opened my door for me before."

"I am not just anybody, I am a somebody and you deserve to have your door opened," I suggested. She took her keys out of her purse, unlocked the door, and stood back while I opened her door. After she sat down in the driver's seat, I closed her door and went to the other side. She reached over and unlocked my door. I looked at her as we drove from the parking lot. "I think you have a good chance of winning Homecoming Queen."

"I don't know. I am sure you know who is going to ask his friends not to vote for me now."

"If they are friends of both of you, I am sure they won't blindly obey him. I don't think his power is as far reaching as you think."

"Has anyone ever told you how wise you are for being such a young person?" Dot asked.

"That has been my problem most of my life. I am always the youngest person in a group where I feel comfortable."

"I didn't mean anything negative; or that you are too young for someone like me," she said, trying to recover from pointing out our age difference.

"I think age is only a number. Wisdom and treatment of people is all about compatibility. We think similarly; we like the same kind of arts (drama and music), and we both like running for relaxation. I think we are good for each other," I concluded as we pulled up to the Dairy Delight.

She turned off the engine and looked over at me. "This is my treat. I need your help," she said. By this time, she was getting out of the car and motioning me to follow her into the Dairy Delight. It was not very busy. She ordered us fries and cokes. I went and claimed a table at the back of the dining room. I sat down and waited for Dot to join me.

Soon she brought our order to the table. "Eat up. It is not every day a lower classman gets treated by a senior," she said with a smile. She continued, "I want this to be a special day for you if you choose to help me out of the predicament in which I find myself."

"I will do whatever you need," I quickly responded.

"I no longer have a date for the dance tomorrow and really don't want to go alone. I don't want it to be awkward for you, and I will understand if you don't feel like you want to go, or that you cannot go with me; but I really, really, would feel proud to go with you."

"You would be proud to be seen with me? Are you kidding; no one will think I am worthy of me being your date for the evening? Are you sure you can risk going with me?"

Eventually we started talking about other things and before we realized it was almost 8:00 p.m. and we needed to leave because it was closing time. As we went back to her car, I felt my world was about to change forever. It was like time had stopped and our talking occupied no time at all. They were the happiest few hours of my life. I told her, "I can walk home; you probably need to get home and you don't even know where I live."

She said, "I don't, but I will soon. Get in the car. You are not going to walk home in the dark." As we pulled out of the parking lot, she took her right hand off the steering wheel and placed it on the console. She said, "Will you hold my hand?" I instantly took hold of her hand. I had never experienced such a rush of electricity and feelings rush up my arm and flow directly into my heart. I didn't know if what I was feeling was love; but if it were, I did not want it to end.

"You have to drive over on the other side of the elementary school. The bad side of the tracks," I said.

"There is no bad side," she whispered. We drove down Rodeo Road to the stop sign at the west end of the school.

"Turn left at the Nazarene Church," I directed. As we turned left, there was the church parking lot. Dot pulled into the lot. She put the car in park and turned off the engine. She looked into my eyes and let go of my hand. She placed her right arm around my neck and drew me near. As I moved closer, I saw her close her eyes as our lips touched. It was a soft kiss. She started to retreat and then it happened again. This time it lasted longer. I now had my right arm up around her shoulder area and was brushing her hair. I didn't think I was breathing. My body had never felt this way before. She pulled back and said, "I liked that. Hope you liked it as much."

I could only mutter, "I did." She then repositioned herself, started the car, and took me home while we continued to hold hands.

That night and the next day, all I could think about was this beautiful senior and how lucky I was. As I was finishing my shift at the snack shack after school, our mutual friend handed me a note. She told me to read it in private. I went to one of the benches outside near the parking lot. No other students were near.

The note read, "Ron, thank you for one of the most enjoyable experiences I ever had. You were and are one of the nicest people I know and like. I was feeling really rejected and down and you made me feel whole again. You are one of the kindest people that God ever put on this earth. You know who called me today and begged me to give him another chance. We have spent almost two years together. I don't know if it will work out, but I feel I need to give it one last try. If it doesn't work out, and you would be willing, I would love to see if what I felt last night is something that could develop. You will always have a special place in my heart and memory. You are going to make someone very happy and feel even more special than you can imagine. Your friend Dot." I did not go to Homecoming that year. In fact, I did not attend any high school dance.

CHAPTER FIVE

It was a Tuesday afternoon in March of my sophomore year that I dropped by Miss Houston's classroom to thank her again for getting me into the speed-reading course. When I entered the room, she was sitting at her desk, blankly staring at a paper in front of her.

"Are you busy?" I asked. She looked up and I could see she was not her usual cheerful self. "I can come back tomorrow if you don't have time to talk now," I said. "You don't happen to know anyone that might want to write a speech on why

"Fighting For Liberty" is so important and can get it memorized by tomorrow at noon do you?" she asked sheepishly.

I replied, "How long does it have to be; and what type of fighting is implied in the subject matter?"

"It is supposed to be six to eight minutes long, and the subject interpretation is really up to the writer. It could be military, volunteer, or some type of service work. I am responsible for having three speakers at the Veterans' Club contest tomorrow at lunch time and one of my three students just cancelled. I have two, but if there are not three student speakers, our winner cannot advance to the semi-final level in Fresno where they could win a $1,500 academic scholarship good for any college the winner chooses," she explained.

I quickly responded, "Anything else I need to know?"

"Well, a parent or guardian has to accompany the speaker. Why, are you suggesting you might be able to help me out?" she asked. "I certainly can write a speech, memorize it, and show up and give it. What I cannot do is bring a parent. I will ask them, but I know that won't happen," I explained.

"Do you have any adult that might accompany you?" she wondered.

"How about you?" I asked.

"Sorry, I am the coordinator. I can't."

I thought for a second. "The pastor of my church might help me out. I can call and ask him."

"We can go to the office and you can use the school phone if you know his phone number," she said as she pushed me toward the classroom door. We went to the office and I called Pastor Robert DeWolfe.

"Pastor DeWolfe, this is Ron Reel. I need to ask a big favor," I said hoping for a positive outcome.

"What is it? I will do what I can, if possible," he said in a very calm manner.

"The school is co-sponsoring a speech contest with the Veterans' Club tomorrow and needs one more speaker, so that there are enough speakers to count as an official contest. I have told my instructor I am willing to enter; but each speaker must have an adult or guardian with them and neither of my parents are able to attend. Do you think you could find it in your heart and schedule to accompany me?" I pleaded.

"I would be honored to accompany you to such a fine outing. My son Larry won the regional Veterans' contest a couple years ago," he stated.

"I have to go home and ask my parents, but so far in my life, only once have they ever attended any function with me. I will call you tonight, but if you can plan on meeting us there it would be greatly appreciated," I explained as I turned back to Miss Houston, who seemed in a better mood.

"I don't expect you to spend most of your evening doing this project. After all, Miss Fresno County and the smartest senior in the history of our school are vying for this scholarship. If you just show up, give a speech, and meet the judges and the Veterans' Club officers, it will set you up to be the odds-on favorite for next year.

Meet me at my classroom at 11:00 a.m. tomorrow and I will drive us to the Clovis Inn," she clarified. I could not let her statement pass without some type of response.

"If I am going to write a speech and memorize it tonight, I am not going to just go through the motion. I plan to be competitive. Well, I won't embarrass myself," I said as I smiled and walked out of the room to go to the library to begin preparing my speech.

On the way to the library, I wondered what it might be like to have Pastor DeWolfe as my father. I would not have to beg him to show up to support me. I could not remember a time when his son, Larry, had been playing football, was the ASB President, was a track star, or was receiving any type of award, when Pastor DeWolfe had not been in attendance; and had always shared those accomplishments with the congregation during a Sunday sermon. He was so proud of his only child; his own son.

I wondered what that felt like. Did that type of love and devotion bring out the best in each of Larry's performances? For just a moment I asked myself what it might be like to be Ronald DeWolfe? His son Larry was one lucky person.

When I got home after going to the library and doing some research on fighting for liberty, I shared with my parents this new opportunity that had developed for me. Momma said, "I am sure you will do a fine job. Your father will be proud too." I then explained that the rules stated that I had to have an adult sponsor attend with me. Momma said, "Neither of us can do that with such short notice. Maybe you can find someone else like Pastor DeWolfe who might enjoy listening to speeches."

I called Pastor DeWolfe and told him he would be needed since my parents could not come to the contest. He said, "Since you need me, I will be there."

I spent most of the evening writing, rewriting, and memorizing my speech. The next day I went to my first three classes. I met Miss Houston at 11:00 a.m. and she had a pass for me to leave with her for the contest. We arrived a few minutes early. Miss Fresno County and her parents as well as Josh Fishman and his parents were already seated. We started toward the other students. Pastor DeWolfe arrived as we were walking to our seats. I was very proud to have him sitting next to me. There had been no talking. Perhaps the other two contestants thought this was my parent. He was dressed in a dark suit and had well-polished shoes. It was the first time I felt encouraged, supported, and loved during any of my public performances.

The master of ceremony had us draw straws for the speaking order. I was the third speaker. I noticed how differently the other two speakers approached the topic. Their approaches were completely different from mine. One discussed military power and the other looked at the topic philosophically; I examined how liberty was the ability to climb out of poverty through education to liberate one from living a life that was less than it could be. As I spoke, I tried to establish eye contact with the judges, various audience members, and from time to time with Pastor DeWolfe. When I completed my speech, I thought the applause was louder and longer than it had been for the other two contestants.

I did not win; I took second place. Pastor DeWolfe told me he thought I should have won. I was happy to hear that because he was a wonderful public speaker. Our church had grown steadily during the years he had been pastor. His sermons were inclusive, full of examples, and he shared with us how we could apply his teaching in our lives and within our community.

Just before we left, we were given the judges' written comments. I put them away and did not read them until after I got home. There were five judges and I had received two first place rankings and three second place rankings. One of the judges who gave me a second-place ranking wrote, "Your content and delivery were superior to the other two students. I had to think long and hard to make my final decision. Because you are so young, you will have two more opportunities to earn scholarships from us. Therefore, I voted for one of the seniors."

I was very disappointed. I think the best speaker should always be recognized regardless of age, sex, how they look, or what they wear. The most important criterion should be how they develop their topic. That judge was correct, however, about one thing. I would have a number of opportunities to win a first-place trophy in the future.

For most students at Clovis High School lunch time meant an opportunity to hang out with their friends, relax for a few minutes from the job of being educated (which is really the job at hand), get some nourishment (fries, burger, burrito, candy, drink), and most importantly just socialize. It was different for me. Because I worked at the Snack Shack, our in-house fast food (not to be confused with any national chain of restaurants), I was released five minutes before the lunch break to give me extra time to arrive at the shack, wash my hands, put on my school-colored blue and gold apron, and stand at one of six windows eagerly waiting to take food orders from other students. For fifty minutes I was able to leave academia and become a business intern paid one dollar per shift and given a free lunch of anything off the menu without limitation. Each of the window interns was expected to take a minimum of sixty orders which was slightly more than one per minute. I had paid attention in my math course.

Most order takers struggle to complete the cycle of greeting the customer, hearing the order, transferring the data to recollection so they can write it on a pad of some sort, repeat it to measure the accuracy, add what was missed, repeat the order, get the product, use the pad and pencil to add each item to arrive at the price to be paid, inform the customer of the amount, accept the initial money exchange, return any surplus money to the customer, thank the customer, and finally repeat actions with the next person in line.

I did not have to write down the orders because I could remember what the customer ordered. I could add the prices in my head as I heard the order being given which allowed me to be the most productive employee every shift. The smarter students migrated to my window because they realized they would be served faster and without error. Some of them thought if they called me by name, they got faster service. That was not the case, but it allowed me an opportunity to make sure I knew their name. If I did not know them, and they called me by name, I would not let them have their food until they told me their name. This game of nametag helped me to know a lot of students.

One day a special student arrived at my window when there were no other students in line for food. She gave me her usual order; after a few times of ordering, I knew exactly what most of my customers were going to order. I noticed she was reading a colorful flyer. She was the reigning Miss Fresno County and we had met at a recent Veterans' Club speech contest. I asked her what she was reading about so intently, and she told me about this speech contest she was thinking of entering. As she turned to leave my window, she handed the flyer to me. I walked over to where I had placed my books and binder and slipped it inside for safekeeping.

After I got home and was doing my homework, I found the flyer. I noticed the initials NFL at the top of the advertisement. It was not the National Football League. It was the National Forensics League, the organization sponsoring the competition. There were quite a few types of competition called categories. These included oratory, extemporaneous speaking, impromptu speaking, informative speaking, dramatic interpretation, and humorous interpretation. I was taking a drama class and had just done a scene from "Of Mice and Men" for a class assignment. Mr. Mason, my drama teacher, had given me an A+ grade and told me the two voices I gave George and Lenny were amazing. That assignment was a scene that lasted six minutes.

This flyer said you could take a scene from a book, novel, or play for the dramatic scene. The time-limit for the presentation was to be from eight to ten minutes including an introduction. I figured I could add an introduction and a few more lines and I would have my selection. I was intrigued by a second discovery from the flyer. The competition was going to be held at Clovis High School in two weeks on a Saturday. The flyer also indicated there were three levels or divisions of expertise for the competition. Novice division was for beginners, Junior division was for freshmen and sophomores, and Senior division was for advanced competitors. I thought I would try the Novice division since I had never participated. The flyer informed participants to contact the appropriate faculty member at the schools to sign up.

The next day I went to the office to ask who at Clovis High School was the faculty member responsible for the forensics program. I found out we did not have an official faculty member coaching because we did not have a team. Miss Houston, my speed-reading instructor, who had accompanied me to the Veterans' Club contest, had been appointed as the advisor. She was coordinating the event if any students were interested in participating. I went to her to seek clarification of how I might participate. I opened the door to her classroom. "I saw this flyer and was wondering how I might enter this contest?" She put down her pen and pushed her chair back as she started our conversation.

"We don't have a formal team yet. I have two other students who are thinking of participating. I think one student might be participating this time. She is going to let me know in the next couple of days. They are keeping her busy as Miss Fresno County. I am trying to get some students to come and observe and if they like what they see, perhaps we will start a team next year. Our school was selected to host the event as a way to generate some in-house publicity. Would you like to come and observe?" she asked.

"I would like to participate in the Dramatic Interpretation category. I have a cutting from "Of Mice and Men" prepared. I did it in my drama class and it got rave reviews. Would you like for me to do it for you?" I asked.

"Well, I would. But today is not a good day. I have an appointment in Fresno within the hour. I have to report to the forensics league officers about how many rooms we have that can be used for the contest and other logistics for the competition. If you can you stop by tomorrow after school, you can show me your presentation."

"Does it cost anything to enter?" I asked. She smiled. "If you are willing and prepared to enter at this late date, the school will pay your entry." I later found out she paid my entry fee herself.

I went back the next day and shared my presentation with Miss Houston. After I finished my scene, she asked,

"Where have you been keeping your acting talent from me this year? I knew you would do well in your other classes after you did so well in mine, but I had no idea what a good actor you would make." I did not know how to respond. I could be seen in the Snack Shack every lunch hour. I could tell she liked my presentation. While I was making my presentation, she seemed engaged and especially during the most emotional part, I thought I saw her wipe away a tear. She stood up and came and hugged me for joy.

"We have to change your introduction ever so slightly. The rules dictate how the material must be introduced so there are no charges of plagiarism or misinterpretation of where the material came from; but besides that, you are the student I have been waiting for this entire year. Here is what you need to do. Don't change anything about the presentation itself. Your voices, the stance, your placement of characters, the intensity and build-up are spot on! Hold the last word for a count of three seconds. Close your eyes and bow your head and count to three, look back at your audience and walk back to your seat. I think...no, I know you are going to win Novice division." We chatted for a few additional minutes about the logistics, where I would meet her, the specific time for me to arrive, but then we came to what she wanted me to do that was impossible. She wanted me to wear a suit. I had to inform her I did not own a suit. We agreed I would wear dark slacks, a white shirt, and some type of sweater.

I arrived at the school Saturday morning ten minutes before my scheduled time. I was supposed to meet Miss Houston at the entry to the student cafeteria. That is the room where all the competitors and coaches were to assemble. I waited and waited. Many teachers and their students arrived within the next twenty minutes. It was now 8:45 a.m. and the competition was to begin at 9:00 a.m. One of the doors leading to the hallway had a sign saying, "Coaches Only." I knocked on the door. A gentleman I did not know came to the door. I asked him if Miss Houston were available for me to see. I thought that perhaps she had gotten busy, was running late, or an emergency had arisen, and she was needed. He turned around and called her name. He came back, "It doesn't look like she is here yet." Almost immediately after he closed the door, another gentleman came out with papers in his hand and taped them to various places along the wall identified as "Postings." I quickly asked a student who was rushing to the wall what all of this meant. He explained to me you are supposed to go to the place on the wall that has the event you are participating in, find your division, locate your student code, go to that room, wait for the judge to arrive, and when your code is called do your presentation. After all the students in that round of competition are finished, you come back and see where you go for the next round and then come back to see where you go for the third round. You compete against different people each round. He told me that once three rounds of competition are over, the top twelve people are advanced to the semifinal round where they compete, and then the final takes the top six people. This was quite a bit to comprehend. Soon all of the students had left the room. I was the only student left. I did not know my code to identify where I was supposed to go.

Again, I knocked on the door. The same man came to the door. I explained who I was and asked again about Miss Houston. Again, he called back into the room asking for her or her whereabouts. A lady came out and inquired why I wanted to see Miss Houston. I explained to her why I was here and needed help with registering for the competition. She directed me to sit down.

"Miss Houston had a car wreck this morning and won't be with us today. If you want to go watch the rounds of competition, I am sure we can arrange for that to take place," she said.

"I am supposed to be competing in the Novice division of Dramatic Interpretation," I explained.

"I don't think Miss Houston entered any students for the competition."

"She told me she called and I...we, met the deadline by one day. Can you check with the person responsible to see if that took place?" I requested. The nice lady retreated to the "Tab Room." She returned and told me, "I have good and bad news for you. Miss Houston did enter you into competition and that is the good news. The bad news is that instead of entering you in Novice, you were entered into the Senior division," she reported.

"Is there any possible way I can be added to the right division?" I asked.

"Not at this late time. I can get your code for you and we can get you to the correct room; and I can make sure the judge listens to your performance if you want to compete. Some of the students you will be competing against have gone to the state and national finals. You may feel intimidated, but I would suggest you use it as a learning opportunity and watch what they do, how they place their characters when using focal points, and pay close attention to their performance techniques. Don't expect to win. Make it all about learning. If you want to proceed, I can get you to the room. You don't have to compete, but if you are going to do so, it must happen now," she said.

"I have prepared and am ready to try," I said. She gave me my secret student code, showed me at the wall how to find the code and the room number where I was to report. I told her I could take us both to the room because this was my school, and I was familiar with the location of all the rooms. As we arrived at the classroom, the door opened, and students began leaving. The nice lady, (she never told me her name), signaled for me to wait. She went into the room and I could see through the window she was having a conversation with the judge. She returned and told me to proceed and deliver my presentation. As I entered the room, the judge said, "Welcome! Do you need to take a couple minutes to get your composure?"

"I think I am ready. I have never been in a contest like this before. My coach was in a car wreck this morning, and if you can tell me where I should stand, I will get started," I explained. He got out of his chair and motioned for me to come to the front of the classroom.

"You always want to come to the front of the classroom or stage when you get to the semi-finals or finals. Eye the center of the audience. Always step back so you have room to move toward your audience once you and the audience have established a relationship. Position yourself where you want to stand. Look at your audience or judges and wait for them to give you a sign to begin. Never start until all members of the audience are giving you their undivided attention." He sat down and I did as he instructed. He seemed to enjoy my performance. Although I did not notice at the time, he must have been writing during most of my presentation. Once it was over, he told me I could leave and instructed me to go back to the posting area and look for Round Two postings and go and wait until it was my turn to repeat my performance.

In my heart, I thought I had made an excellent presentation, but because of my being late, I had not seen any of my competitors. Round Two would allow for me to learn from these senior participants. I got to the room early. I sat towards the back of the room slightly off center. A couple of students arrived. I introduced myself. They introduced themselves. Then one of them said,

"Oh no, guess who is in our round? Mindy of course." I was curious as to why this person was of such concern. I asked, "Who is Mindy and why don't we want her in our round?"

"She was fifth in the state last year and she hopes to win this year." I thought I might learn much from her. I was glad she was to perform. I kept my excitement to myself. My opinion of her changed once she entered and spoke to all of us sitting in the room without a judge.

"Good morning all. Good luck to each of you. You will need it. I am here to win. Learn all you can from me," she graciously and sarcastically stated. I hoped I would go after her so I could learn from her before I had to perform. That did not happen. I was the third speaker; she was the sixth and last performer. She was very good, but so were two other people in our round.

After the third round was over, I thought I had learned quite a bit from the other students. I was getting ready to go look at the posting wall so I could go and watch one of the semi-finals rounds when one of the competitors I had faced in round two came up and congratulated me. I didn't know why. I asked, "What do you mean?"

"You made it to the semi-finals. Congratulations!" he said. I went to the posting wall and looked. My code was posted in Room 7 and I was Speaker 6. Much excitement was taking place in the room. Coaches from the various schools were out in the room hugging, congratulating, and some were giving pointers to their students. I was alone. I was happy I had made it to the elimination round. Part of me thought perhaps a mistake had taken place. I didn't know what to do. I saw the nice lady who had helped me earlier. She was talking with two of her students. I waited until she told them good luck and sent them off to their rounds. I tapped her on her shoulder. As she turned around, I spoke, "I just wanted to thank you for helping me this morning. I apologize, but I don't even know your name."

"I coach at South Fresno High. What was your name?"

"My name is Ron Reel. Can I ask one more question?"

"Of course, but before you do, can you tell me what you learned most from all the senior students?

"I learned much about the performance. Some of those students are like watching professional actors," I shared.

"I am glad you were able to learn. I hope you didn't feel inferior. Remember, you are just starting. Some of them have been doing this for years. Now what did you want to know?"

"When you go to the semifinal and final round, do you change your performance in any way, or do you just keep doing it the same way?"

'I always tell my student to adjust volume to the size of the room. The elimination rounds are always in larger rooms. We don't make changes once the tournament starts. We wait until after the tournament and read the comments from the judges to see what worked and what needs improving. You are asking the right questions. Stick in there and you might have a future in this activity. Are you going to go watch one of the semifinal rounds?" she asked.

"I am going to go to one of them, but not to watch but to compete," I said as I turned to walk to the room. I could hear her trying to recover and I think I remember her saying, "Good luck." She never did reveal her name.

About forty-five minutes after the semifinal rounds were completed the list of six finalists was posted. One by one I saw the contestants go and look to see if their code was listed as a finalist. Mindy had several people around her as she went to the posting board. She was writing down the codes. Her friends were congratulating her. As they walked past me, she looked directly at me and said, "They must have made a mistake. Congratulations to you. One less person I have to worry about."

I now had to go to the posting wall. Sure enough, my code was posted. I took a deep breath and slowly walked toward the auditorium, which seated five hundred people. This was where our final round would be held. As I turned toward it, I heard someone shouting my name. I turned and found Miss Houston was doing her best to get to me on crutches. She had broken her leg and it was in a cast, and I could see bruises on her arms. She spoke first, "The other coaches just told me you made finals. What an honor your first time out in Novice competition."

"Finals, yes! Novice division, No! They made me compete in Senior Division!" I said. She screamed again louder and more energetically than before.

"What?"

"Yeah."

"Do you mind if I come and watch?" she asked.

"I don't have anyone else. I would love for you to be there with me. If it were not for you, I would not be here," I said. Everyone in the final round was amazing. After the round was over, Miss Houston shared with me that two of the students in the final round had been California State finalists the year before. I did not win. I took second place. Even though I did not win that contest, I now knew I had found something I really wanted to do for the rest of my high school career. As it turned out, I spent a number of years coaching this activity at both the high school and college levels.

My sophomore year at Clovis High School was turning into one of the best years of my young life. In addition to starting a forensics program, the school was having a talent contest. I was singing in the school choir that semester as one of my electives. Some of the very confident and outgoing soloists announced they would be participating. One of my friends encouraged me to show off my singing talent. I checked the rules regarding the singing competition. All soloists had to have a live accompanist. I did not know a single person who could meet that requirement. My circle of friends was quite small. One of the Anderson brothers, Mark, in my Advanced Spanish class, had an older brother who played the piano. His name was Steve and he had graduated the year before. I had heard him play at various functions from jazz band to Sunday morning service at the First Methodist Church. Mark told me he thought his brother would accompany me if I wanted to enter the contest. To make a somewhat long story shorter, Mark volunteered Steve, who had been very well liked at school. Steve and I met and practiced a couple of times. I was singing the song "Tammy," although I had never heard it sung by a male performer.

The night before the contest, as we were practicing, I realized I did not have any appropriate clothing to wear. Steve suggested I wear a sweater like Andy Williams wore for his television appearances. I did not own such a sweater. The next day, however, as the contestants arrived for the final rehearsal, he had a surprise for me. He loaned me the most beautiful sweater I had ever seen at that time in my life, or since. But even that sweater might not be enough to save me. Many felt the contest was already decided because the same girl, who had won it the last three years, was now a senior and, perhaps, the best majorette in the entire valley. This year she was going to twirl three batons that were literally on fire. I was the sixth contestant. When I heard the announcer call my name, I stood behind the main stage curtain taking a couple deep breaths before I started walking toward the piano; there was not much applause. I did hear some students begin to talk and giggle. I don't think they were necessarily laughing at me because most of them did not know me. The spotlight suddenly was focused on Steve as he walked to the piano. The audience erupted in applause. He went to the center of the stage, sat down, and gestured toward me to join him. He started to play and there was absolute silence in the auditorium. I opened my mouth and out came a baritone voice none were expecting. I felt I captured Andy Williams in my performance. When I finished my song, there was an instant standing ovation from the audience. I basked for what seemed like a few minutes in total acceptance, appreciation, and most importantly, connection with other human beings. I did not win. The baton twirler won for the fourth straight year.

CHAPTER SIX

By the time I was a junior, I knew I wanted to attend college. What I didn't know was how I could afford to finance such an enormous undertaking. I knew running was not going to be my way out. I had heard of academic scholarships for going to college. Not many of the students I knew from any of the three high schools I attended were going to college on scholarships. Most were being sent to college by their parents, who were paying their way. Most of the middle-class students had secured a combination of finances that included scholarships, student loans, and family support. A friend had told me I might qualify for a government loan to attend college. He said this type of loan would be forgiven if I would work in certain impoverished areas after completing my degree. I thought that might work. I was told that if I returned to the central valley and worked for so many years, the loan would be forgiven.

I needed to find someone who could not only help explain the college application process to me, but who could also help me with completing the actual applications, writing, and submitting the completed paperwork. I found out that some students were using a woman who seemed to have an outstanding reputation and a successful completion record for her clients. Only one thing stood between her helping me and my success. She charged one hundred dollars. That was about ninety-nine dollars more than I had. Nevertheless, I asked one of my teachers if she could arrange an introductory appointment for me to meet Mrs. Huckleberry.

Just before school was out for the summer, my appointment with Mrs. Huckleberry took place. During this meeting she explained about scholarships, internships, work-study programs, sponsorships, benefactors, regular governmental student loans, and then finally the student forgiveness loans. There were scholarships based on your parent's race, occupation, income, service to the country (VA), and even family name. Some merit scholarships were based on your gradepoint average, type of classes you completed, activities you joined, and recommendations from teachers willing to write letters of support for you. One thing she told me shocked me: millions of dollars' worth of scholarships each year go unused because students do not apply for them.

At the end of our meeting, Mrs. Huckleberry asked me a few additional questions about my grades, accomplishments, activities, and what colleges I was considering. I told her I needed some time to compose the answers to those questions and asked her if we could schedule another meeting after I had time to digest the information she had shared. She informed me we could meet again in about a week. She then said something about how she was going to be paid for her services.

I thought she asked me who would be paying for the services she would be providing for me. That was one of the most difficult moments of my life. I realized I really needed her help. I realized I did not have the ability to do the work by myself. I realized why so few students from my community ever had the opportunity to go to college. I also realized I did not have the means to pay for her services.

I looked directly into her eyes, establishing as much direct communication as possible and said, "I know what you can do for me is much more than I deserve. I now understand why some of the students call you the "Miracle Worker." I thought I could do this on my own, and only need a bit of help. But after our meeting, I know your services will make the difference between my going to college and probably not going because I cannot imagine doing all that needs to be completed. I don't even know where to start," I said as I took a deep breath. She interrupted me, "Ronald, I wanted you to guess who has *already* paid me to accept you as a client. I was making sure you knew that Miss Houston in the English Department, your newest favorite teacher, has already paid me my fee."

I was suddenly overcome. This was the third time Miss Houston had done me a great service. The first time she had gone to the principal my freshman year and convinced him to allow me to be enrolled in a speed-reading course she was teaching to a group of seniors. I don't know how she did it; but I would take the results of that class with me into my adult life. The average American reads about 100-200 words per minute. During that semester, I went from about 150 words per minute to over 1,000 words per minute with about 90% comprehension. Getting me into her course was invaluable to me. The second time she used her own funds to enter me into an interpretation contest. Paying Mrs. Huckleberry for me would help me get a college education. My eyes filled with tears of joy and appreciation. The fact that another human being cared enough for me to do something like this was mindblowing.

Speed reading allowed me to work full-time and carry an average of 20 units each semester of college. It allowed me to have my Master of Arts Degree before I was twenty-three years old. Since that day, I have paid forward to students needing financial assistance, whenever the time arose, and I was able to assist. Because someone believed in me, I have been able to believe in others. My church also played a major role in my earning a college degree.

During the summer vacation of my junior year the church offered two scholarships; one each to a barber college and to a cosmetology college. I wanted to attend a major college or university and I knew it would be my own responsibility to meet all the other financial obligations that occur in addition to the books and tuition that Mrs. Huckleberry would help me obtain. My family was not in a position where they could help at all.

The church awarded me one of the scholarships. The nephew of an influential family who attended the church came to live with them. He wanted to follow in the footsteps of his uncle, who owned one of the two successful barber shops in town. While I wanted to go to barber college with the hopes of earning money to get further schooling, it did not happen. The nephew was given that scholarship. I was told I could have the cosmetology scholarship.

Perhaps because it was 1967, it felt strange to be a seventeen-year-old boy going to a cosmetology college. Even though I had five sisters, I had never paid attention to how they had braided, teased, or colored their hair. I had never placed a roller or tried to style their hair. It was all I could do to comb my own hair after it got cut.

The cosmetology training was an opportunity I could not let pass. My church wanted to give me the vocational training I would need to change the course of my life. One of the saving graces of the situation as far as I was concerned was the fact one of the instructors at the cosmetology college was a man who had dated my older sister Nellie. I only knew he cut hair, but I soon learned that he was an awardwinning hair cutter who charged so much per cut that no one in my family could afford to have him cut their hair. He had his own salon where he worked in the evenings and on weekends. He charged $25 dollars for a haircut. Our barber charged $1. I remember my older siblings teasing Nellie who had dated him as being crazy for not staying with him. He now had a wife and several children and lived in a nice part of Fresno.

I respected his masculinity, and I didn't feel as threatened once I found out he was the guest cutting specialist at my new school. If Danny Denton was a legitimate hair stylist and renowned hair cutter, I could follow in his footsteps. Well, at least I convinced myself I could try.

I did not know how I would get from Clovis to downtown Fresno five days a week. Clovis is located eight miles from downtown Fresno. When I called to schedule an interview with the administrator of the cosmetology school, she informed me that sometimes several people from the same community would carpool together to cut down on expenses. She knew of several people in the Clovis area who would be attending my school that semester. She suggested I talk with them.

I found out that two older women (they were in their late twenties or early thirties) were starting the same time I was and would be traveling back and forth from Clovis. I contacted them and they allowed me to sit in the back seat of their automobile each day for one dollar of gas per week. At that time gasoline sold for twenty cents per gallon.

I had no idea of the ridiculing and cruelty that I would soon encounter because of my acceptance of that scholarship to attend cosmetology college. When I was at the "beauty college" I felt fine. Outside of school, however, I was the butt of a lot of jokes and even suffered harassment.

My first day at the beauty college was one of the most embarrassing days of my life. If only I had known then what I have learned since, my insecurity about myself and worry about my ability to succeed in a profession, which I knew nothing about, might not have been so taxing on my nerves. Our beginning class had thirty-three students: thirty girls and three boys. It was interesting to me there were only two other guys in the class. The entire beauty school had 100 students: ninety-three girls and seven boys. The odds of securing a girlfriend appeared quite promising. During the next year I would discover that some of these girls were very different from the girls I had known in my college prep classes at the various high schools I had attended. They appeared to be hardened, loud, assertive, and they cursed louder and more often than I had ever heard from boys or men. Yet, this generalization did not hold true for all. My class also held a few delicate and sensitive women who displayed the finest qualities of femininity. They too were assertive when it came to hairstyling, but they were discreet, savvy, methodic, and focused on obtaining their goals and ambitions.

When looking back to that first day, I can smile now. Then I was too scared to smile. While we "new recruits" as we were called, waited to begin our induction into the world of high fashion hairstyling, it was evident we were "rookies." Our white uniforms were "really white" and new. Our shoes polished to glow. We stood together carrying our suitcases which they had presented us full of rollers, combs, brushes, scissors, tint, shampoo capes, clippers, and our theory book. I was so thankful for the theory book.

I had arrived very early the first day. School did not begin until 8:00 a.m. I arrived at 7:00 a.m. Sarah and Darlene, who provided my transportation, wanted to make sure we arrived early so they could be the first two admitted into the building on the first day. They told me it was like animals establishing territory markers. They both smoked. Standing outside the building at the end facing F Street, they started to smoke. I went to the other end of the building to get away from the cigarette smell. When they finally opened the doors, we spent the morning registering for school. We had to fill out forms, take some tests examining our ability to recognize shapes and objects, tour the facility, and introduce ourselves to one another. During the afternoon practice session, I proved to be the clumsiest hairdresser ever to step foot into the world of hair design.

I could not get a roller to stay on the mannequin in front of me. It kept sliding out and falling onto the floor. I thought I was getting in over my head; this career was too much for me. Two girls, who had been doing each other's hair, began to laugh at me. "Hey, why don't you get some glue and put it on the roller," suggested the blonde. "Maybe you could get the hair to stay around the roller with Elmer's Glue," added the redhead. The blonde closed the conversation, "Just give it up and go home," she said.

I kept right on trying. By late afternoon, we had progressed from rolling hair with rollers to finger waving. This maneuver was even more frightening. Each student was expected to make the mannequin's hair wave on each side of its head. The instructor's concept of "wave" went way beyond the capability of "Hair Designs" by Ronald. My mannequin looked like there was no wind on the sea that day. The waves were only ripples.

The instructor found good things to say about the hair waves of everyone except me. She was a kind lady, but she could not find any nice things to say about my hair design. After she had us put our mannequins away, cleaned up, and reminded us to read the first chapter of the text for the theory class the next day, she dismissed the entire class. Well, she asked me to stay behind. As she walked toward me, she smiled, "Ron, I overheard a couple of the girls today. I watched how hard you concentrate. You need to relax. It will all come to you in time."

"I guess I just don't have what it takes," I admitted with great embarrassment. That afternoon may have been the first time in my life I could not figure out how to complete a task I was given. I was very uneasy in a very uncomfortable environment. I wanted this to be some type of academic challenge or memorization of facts competition so I could feel at least equal to others in the same situation. This was all so foreign to me.

"You have a big decision to make tonight. You're going to get home and assess whether all of this unfamiliar territory is worth it. Those dropped rollers and the stiffness in the finger waves will all be mastered in the course of time. The tests you took this morning indicate you are very capable of learning what will look good on your patrons," she ended her sentence by placing an encouraging hand on my shoulder.

"I feel so helpless," I said. She could tell I was desperately trying to make a decision whether to run or to stay and fight for survival. I needed to hear something positive regarding my ability to succeed.

"Look, if you asked me to work on my car today, I would feel the same way. Just because you don't know now, doesn't mean you can't learn. It is going to take hard work; a lot of it. I bet you are used to good old hard work, aren't you?" She asked.

"OK, I'll think about it," I said as I walked toward the exit door. My inner self was trying to convince me not to return. That would be the easiest and most comfortable thing to do. Why would I want to embarrass myself in an occupation that would bring many unique challenges to an already questionable quest to climb from one environment (poverty) to another (college educated) for someone my age who did not have any family direction, support, or role modeling. Going to college would be more than a challenge. Trying to accomplish this task to use as a steppingstone to get there might be more than I could handle. I did not feel able to continue.

"I hope you decide to stay. I am betting you will be one of our best," said Mrs. Norden.

Sarah and Darlene were waiting for me when I got to the car. It seemed to take a very long time to arrive home that day. They talked continually about how wonderful the experience had been on this first day of their adventure. Neither asked how my day had gone. They were there in the classroom. They did not have to ask.

They had lived that horrible day right beside me. When they finally dropped me off, one of them said as they drove away, "See you in the morning." I don't think she really thought that would happen.

When I got home, Momma greeted me with a big smile and great curiosity.

"Did you learn to do hair?" she asked.

"Sure," I replied, but I think she could see that something was wrong.

"Well, why don't you practice each night on me? You know how I love to have my hair fooled with. If I am your model, you can practice each and every step you need to learn," she offered in a very caring manner.

"You mean it?" I eagerly asked. Perhaps this was my solution. If I could practice additional hours every single day, I might have a chance to succeed. I had always heard the slogan that practice makes perfect. What if it really worked?

"Sure! You know, you can do anything you set your mind to!" She was happy to help.

That first night I practiced finger waves on the sides of her head until they looked passable. I stood back and exclaimed, "Those are good finger waves! Mrs. Nordon said real people were easier to work on than mannequins. She was right!"

Momma looked puzzled. "Well, aren't ya gonna do something with the top?" she asked.

"Oh...Uh...we...we learn that tomorrow," I stammered.

"You mean I have to go around looking like this all day tomorrow?" she asked in a loud voice pretending to be angry. She started to laugh. Then we both laughed because she sat with a half-finished hairdo. From that day on her hair was always styled by me. Those early days were tedious, and she wore awkward styles, but soon her hair began to look the way I had wanted it coiffured for some time.

I read my theory book each evening. After all, it was a textbook. It explained the theory behind cosmetology. Not many people realize the theoretical implications behind the construct of hair design. The understanding of chemicals used in coloring, straightening, and giving additional curl (perms) fascinated me. I had never taken art in school. Achieving different shades of brown, red, golden blond and platinum blond had never concerned me. I had not even known there were varying shades of black. I had so much to learn. The academic implications were a breeze for me. It was the practical learning how to style hair that was problematic.

The fact that human hair drilled into a mannequin is more difficult to manage than hair in a real scalp was difficult for me to grasp. There was short hair, medium length hair, and various lengths of long hair. There was fine textured hair, medium, and coarse hair. Some hair was straight while some hair was very curly. The difference in setting hair (using rollers of various sizes) to gain additional curl or to loosen the curl was fascinating. Placing rollers on angles created direction to one side or another. Placing a roller directly over, exaggerating it on top, or stretching to the front caused a different result. The use of hair gel and the amount and density of it proved to be an art of its own.

I soon realized that no two people have the exact same type of hair. Even twins have different growing planes of hair. It was exciting to learn how the hair of each side of your head is different in texture, amount, and the direction. The speed at which it grows is also very different. Some people have hair that grows toward their face. Other people have hair that flows away from their face. Some have hair in the back of the head called the nape area that grows up, down, or sideways. One soon learns that adjustments in length and the use of scissors, a straight razor, or clippers results in different ways the hair will lay for different types of styles. So many barbers of old just used hair clippers that cut all the hair off evenly around the entire head. This is not the cosmetologist's way. He or she uses a combination of approaches. Even the "clippers" have various styling attachments for various levels of cutting and styling. Proper cutting is not only a science; it is also an art. Cosmetology College taught me that raw talent does not have to remain raw; but can be developed by a good teacher. When one learns the basic concepts, applications, and positioning of instruments, one becomes knowledgeable and capable.

Some of the situations I found myself in because of being a male attending beauty college were not as amusing at that time as now. The older I get, the more amusing they appear. One day I went out into the lobby at the beauty college to call my next patron. There was only one lady sitting there and she was about sixty-five years old, small-framed, attentive, alert, and very much alive.

"Mrs. Bowman," I said. There was no answer. I thought perhaps she had not heard me. She looked like she could be anyone's grandmother. I thought it strange she did not make any body movement after my speaking to her. She sat looking straight ahead.

"Mrs. Bowman?" I repeated as I moved directly in front of her. I bent down slightly to look directly into her eyes. "My name is Ron. I am supposed to do your hair today," I stated. She sat there as though she could not or would not hear me. She still did not move. She showed no reaction to me at all.

I went back and told Mrs. Nordon, my supervisor, that either Mrs. Bowman was not out in front, or the woman I was trying to communicate with didn't want me to do her hair. Mrs. Nordon took me by the hand and led me back to the lobby.

"Mrs. Bowman, this student is waiting to do your hair," she said, recognizing this woman who had been there before.

Mrs. Bowman looked up at Mrs. Nordon and motioned for her to move closer to her so she didn't have to speak loudly. Evidently this was the woman I was supposed to be helping. In the tiniest of voices Mrs. Bowman whispered to my supervisor, "No man is going to do my hair."

I started to get upset. She did not know how good or bad my styling would be before I had a chance to prove myself. I felt ready and able to do whatever was needed to give her the kind of transformation her hair needed. "Why don't you want me to do your hair?" I asked. I felt torn. I was upset with her because she, for whatever reason, did not want me to provide my services. At the same time, I wanted her to be happy. Most of all, I wanted to find out why she was so strongly refusing to let me do her hair.

"My husband and I know about male cosmetologists," she said smugly.

"What is it that you know?"

"They charge more money just because they are a man! He is going to charge me more money than any of the girls would," she said.

I would never charge more just because I am a male. Besides, the school charges the client based on the service not on the person who did the job. Because of this attack on my personal character, I had to stand up to her. "I am sorry you feel this way, Mrs. Bowman. I would never charge anyone more because she was a woman. I will pray for you tonight. In fact, I will pray for you the rest of my life. It is people like you who are hindering other people from being what they want to be; I believe in equal pay for equal work. You will pay the same whether I cut your hair or one of the female students," I retorted.

"What do you mean, you'll pray for me?" she questioned.

"I mean that I will be attending Trinity University in the fall, and I hope to be a minister someday and preach to people like you. We are all equal. Men and women should be treated the same. If you do the same work; you deserve to be paid the same."

Mrs. Bowman had another question, "Do you mean you are a Christian?"

"Yes, Mrs. Bowman, I am a Christian, and I will pray for you each and every day." I turned to walk away. Suddenly Mrs. Bowman wanted to carry on a conversation with me. "What church do you attend?" she asked.

"I don't see there is any reason for disclosing that to you, but I attend God's Holy Assembly."

"Praise the Lord! I prayed last night whether or not to come back here to have my hair done. The Lord told me to return here. Now, I know why! Come young man," she said as she took hold of my tunic and placed her arm around mine.

"We must get my hair done because time is wasting. If you are not charging more, than it doesn't really matter who does my hair." Mrs. Bowman became a standing appointment every week until I graduated from the college. God, however, did not tell her to follow me out into the world of hair design after I had graduated. The cost of having her hair done professionally whether by me or a female licensed professional was substantially more than what she paid at the beauty college and she was not willing to pay anyone more.

One Saturday night my friend Tom and I went to Fresno to see a movie. Tom

Betencourt's parents allowed him to drive their new car from Clovis into Fresno. His parents were quite wealthy. I knew him from being in a play that semester. We were doing "Winnie the Pooh" for children's theatre. He played Christopher Robin in the show. I played Tigger. We were dragging Blackstone Boulevard when he noticed a car with two girls, who had pulled up beside us. He motioned for me to look at them. He rolled down his window and started a conversation.

"Girls, roll down your window. What are you doing out tonight?" he asked. One of the girls answered him quickly and firmly. "We're just out looking for some fun. You looking for some fun?" she asked. I recognized the voice. I knew it was a girl from the beauty school whom I had nicknamed "Juicy" because she was usually chewing a large wad of *Juicy Fruit* gum to cover up her breath which often smelled like she had been drinking. Of all the hairstylists at the college, she was the most confrontational with the instructors and her patrons. She had been suspended for one week and some of us thought it might have been for showing up to school after a long night of partying and drinking. Tonight, the gum was missing; but I was confident she probably had been drinking. Before I could explain anything to Tom, I heard the other girl, a very pretty redhead, speak up: "We thought you boys might want to get together," she said. I recognized that voice as well; but it was not the voice of a real girl. It was the feigned voice of one of the guys from the beauty college, now dressed as a girl. Tonight, they looked like two typical girls cruising Blackstone. Had it not been these two particular girls, we would have been lucky to have such pretty girls vying for our attention. Now, however, I had no idea how to handle the situation.

By this time the duo in the car recognized me. "Hi Ron," the redhead called from the passenger seat. He waved her hands with great excitement and he kept his feminine voice.

Both began to laugh, "Imagine meeting you here on Blackstone," said Juicy. Tom looked at me wondering what was going on.

"You know these girls? Let's divide up. I'll take the redhead. You take the brunette," he said. Tom started to motion for them to pull over to the side of the street. He felt our luck with pretty girls was about to change. I looked at him with shock and suggested a different kind of action: "Hit the gas and let's get out of here," I said. I whispered each word, trying to say it loud enough for him to hear but not loud enough for the other cars passengers to know what I wanted to do.

Tom thought he had a better idea: "What are you talking about? This is what we have dreamed would happen to a couple guys like us. Man up and let's see what will happen."

I realized I had to reveal to him what I knew about the other car's passengers "Those girls are not what you think. I know them from the beauty college," I said.

He turned and smiled at me. "That's even better. They probably have more experience than anyone else we know. Maybe this is our lucky night." By this time, they were pulling over to the side of the street, motioning for us to pull over as well.

"Come on, let's have some fun together," called out the redhead beauty. I looked directly at Tom and blurted out something he was not expecting.

"The redhead is a guy," I said. Tom looked at me in disbelief.

"Really, you are going to sink to this kind of statement. Are you saying this because you think she is too good for me? She is hot. She is not a guy."

"The girl you want is really guy," I said again. This time my statement was firm; I stressed each word so Tom could hear I meant what I was saying.

"As long as you know that upfront, we can do this if you want," I added.

"How can that be?" Tom asked. He was completely convinced the redhead was a girl. He had never seen a cross dresser or female impersonator.

"She is really beautiful. Are you sure you are not jealous; because I think I want her? Or do you want to switch girls? I am OK if you want to do that," he said.

"I don't want to change anything except the direction we are headed. Don't pull over. Keep going. Let's get out of here. I will explain more about them later. Go!" He complied reluctantly.

I had learned much during my summer months. My world had been opened to a very different world from the one I had known previously. I was only seventeen and had never experienced the situation like the one

I had just had with Tom. Fortunately, Tom decided I was telling him the truth about the girls cruising Blackstone. Neither of us looked back. Tom pulled into the fast lane and we sped off to find the movie theatre where we were headed originally. Neither of us talked about the incident for the rest of the evening. In fact, we never mentioned it again.

I should have handled the awkward situation differently. I should have immediately told the two people in the other car that we were on our way to the movies and did not have time then to stop and talk. I could have suggested that we meet up together some other time (after I had the chance to explain the situation to Tom). I just knew neither Tom nor I was ready for our first exposure to such a possibility at this time in our lives. I had been very naive until the summer of 1967, and Tom had been sheltered by his parents more than I. It was my first experience with that kind of situation, and I was not prepared to do the right thing. I had not supported either of the two individuals from the beauty college. I should have recognized their right to be the persons they wanted to be at that moment.

On the following Monday the two of them tried to shame me for not pulling over and meeting up with them. I did not mean to hurt them, and I tried to explain that my friend Tom was not prepared to meet them that evening. As I reflect on the situation today, I know I could have handled it better. As a society, we have finally begun to accept people as they are. I am glad we are more accepting now. Tom was even more innocent in worldly things than I was at the time.

Summer came to an end too soon. As I returned to regular high school, I felt much older than any of the other students my age because of my adventure into becoming a male student at a beauty college.

CHAPTER SEVEN

Momma had become very ill in late July of 1967. We had taken her to a doctor in Selma, but he had not been able to figure out what was wrong. He put Momma on "exploratory" medications. We later found out that term had been used because he was trying to find out what was wrong with her by giving her different kinds of medication to see if any of them would help. We all hoped he could find the right one soon. From week to week, new medicines and new side effects showed up.

One day when we took Momma for her scheduled appointment, we found the doctor's office had been boarded up and a sign hung over the entrance which said he had moved to Millerton Lake, too many miles from our home to make visits possible. Without a doctor to give Momma her medications, her health took a downward spiral quickly. She suddenly was weaker and more fragile than ever. She no longer had medicine and no doctors were taking "our" type of patients for at least six weeks out. In desperation we took Momma to the St. Luke's Hospital Emergency Room. They immediately ran tests on her, and she was admitted for a precautionary examination. The doctors decided she had hepatitis. She had lost a lot of weight recently. She was too weak to continue working in the fields. She was worried about not being able to work because we depended on her additional salary to make ends meet. I tried to comfort her by telling her I would secure an additional job on my own. All of us worked before school and after school whenever possible. I hoped I could find time in the evenings or weekends to help.

In the fall of 1967, I returned to Clovis High School, where I worked in the student store before school, at lunch, and after school to earn extra money. I turned over each of my checks to my parents. They never had to ask for them. I was doing my part to help support the family.

I wanted to end my high school years as one of the members of the top crosscountry team in the valley. Our coach had us running long distances in order to build up our stamina. By the time I got home at around 5:30 p.m., I was exhausted, but chores and responsibilities did not vanish simply because I was tired. Momma was no longer working in the fields but could do little to help in the home. The rest of us were forced to learn to do the house chores that most people take for granted. Traditional roles had been set aside; family responsibility knew no age nor gender. Each of us knew how to cook, do laundry, clean dishes, clean the house, and shop at the store for food. Every time Momma would be home from the hospital, a few days, she always got worse. She would then go to the emergency room and the doctors would readmit her.

Meanwhile the league cross country meet was two weeks away. Coach Silverstone had us working on endurance and sprints. The top five runners had to run long distance sprints morning and afternoons. Our drills were paying off. We were considered one of the top four or five distance relay teams in the entire state.

Coach told us we could win the meet if we would adopt a "no limitations" philosophy. He meant we had to convince ourselves that we could do anything including winning at the state meet. The last dual meet of the season before the league finals was at Kerman. It was just between that school and us. Our distance runners were superior. None of the other schools in Fresno County could compete with the depth we had. Our top four milers were ranked in the top ten to fifteen in the entire state. The next four of us were, depending on the day, temperature, and course were running about five to ten seconds behind them. Coach felt we could take all top five places at tomorrow's final dual meet. He told us we might even get the top eight. That would mean each one of our runners would beat each of the runners from the other school. It had never been done. "We are restrained mostly by our own limitations. If we think we cannot run faster, we won't!" he told us.

My home life had become so difficult that I tried to put in as many hours on the track as possible. While running, I concentrated only on technique and breathing properly. I could push my family and its problems out of my mind for this short time.

That evening I arrived home later than usual. As I walked through the living room door, the atmosphere was tense and unhappy. My sister Karen was crying. She sat on the sofa beside Momma. Her hands covered most of her face. I could tell this scene had been going on for some time. Karen was speaking, "Momma, I know you said I was too young, but that doesn't help. Kevin said he likes someone else!" Momma looked at my sister and did her best to comfort her.

"Karen," she said. "You're going to experience many more feelings like this. You can't let what happens in the mind of someone else hurt you. As you grow older, there will be many young men who look attractive at first; but for some reason that attraction you have for them will change. Or the attraction they have for you will change."

Karen tried to restrain herself. "But Momma, it hurts to think he likes someone else," she said as she began to cry again.

"Hush dear. You'll wake your father," Momma warned as she tried comforting her by hugging her and brushing her hair from her face.

"I can't stop!" Karen cried out louder than before. Suddenly the closed door to my parents' room opened.

"Why is there so much noise out here?" asked Father. Momma was quick to reply.

"It's nothing Bill. You go ahead and go back to bed. I can handle this," she said. At this moment however, Karen blurted out the following words,

"Daddy, I'm sorry, but I just can't stop crying. It hurts," she said. Father looked puzzled.

"What hurts girl?" he asked. Momma quickly responded,

"Oh, nothing Bill. Close the door. I'll get this settled right now." Momma tried to assist Father back to bed, while at the same time, clueing my sister with a hand gesture to calm down.

"But Momma, it hurts," Karen repeated yet again. By this time, Father decided to take control of the situation the only way he knew in his limited family discipline training. He escalated the situation immediately.

"Karen if you don't shut up crying, I'll give ya somethin to cry about," he said as he moved toward her. Momma was trying to force Father back into the bedroom by closing the door on him and standing directly between him and his daughter.

Karen cried out, "You can't silence my feelings. I hurt and I have to cry. It is only natural for me to have these feelings," she insisted.

Father was not about to have his authority challenged in the home where he presided. "You want somethin that'll really make you cry little girl?" he asked. Karen was not paying attention to any of the clues to pull back or silence her cries, which Momma was offering her.

"Daddy, don't you remember being young? Didn't you ever cry?" Karen kept digging herself in deeper. This was definitely the wrong thing to say. She knew Father had never been allowed to cry. We all had heard the story about how Grandpa Reel made Father go to the corner of a room when he had misbehaved and stand on one leg with his nose in the corner until he was told to move again. If he cried or made any noises, he had time added to his punishment.

"Here, let me give you somethin to cry fer!" said Father, as he pulled back his arm. Momma got between them. The fight had started. Frances, the youngest family member, was now perched on the arm of the sofa watching attentively.

"Bill, I don't think that is necessary. Karen, apologize to your Father," requested Momma.

"I can't Momma. I ache all through my entire body," exclaimed Karen. Father could not tolerate any more disobedience from Karen. He walked into the kitchen and brought back a butcher knife. He then walked over and took the iron away from the ironing board. He cut the cord from the iron. The look he had in his eyes was brutal.

I found myself pleading to Momma. "Quick, take the girls and leave. Momma, go. He's drunk. Get outside. I will stop him!" I said as I ran to intervene. Momma raised her voice and commanded the girls to run outside.

"Karen and Frances leave now! Your Daddy is mad, and I don't want you hurt. He doesn't mean to hurt us, but he just loses his temper. Quick, get out! Run! Now!" she commanded. I walked toward Father.

"I don't think anything like this needs to happen. If you whip Karen with that cord, she'll be crying much worse than she is now," I pleaded.

"Ronald, you get out of my way. This ain't none of your business," he said. "Why do you think you have to get involved?" he yelled as he moved toward me.

"Father, come on, she's been hurt by her first boyfriend. It's puppy love. She'll stop crying. We can get her to stop. Just go back to sleep. We won't make any noise that will disturb you," I promised.

"You think you have the right to interfere in everything don't ya? I said it ain't none of your business. You ain't the parent. I am," he said as he raised his voice and moved closer toward me.

"I am going to make it my business," I said in the most calming voice I could muster while at the same time being terrified of what was about to take place. "Well then, maybe, you should get the whippin instead," he said in a controlled and solid voice.

I looked straight into his eyes. "If you have to beat somebody, then I'd just as soon it be me instead of the girls or Momma this time," I said.

Father stepped back and doubled the cord. He started hitting my face with the ironing cord. I turned quickly so the blows would land on my back and neck instead.

"I'll beat you and then give them what's comin," he said as he hit me again. Momma was standing at the front door to the house watching. There was a gaze of disbelief that had overcome her while she saw her husband beginning to beat her son. Tears were streaming down her cheeks.

I screamed at her, "Momma, close the door. You and the girls leave, please." Father was now standing behind me. I was imagining this was being done in the same manner as the man who whipped Christ had stood. The next blow hit my back squarely in the middle. My spine seemed to crack sharply as the cord ripped through my shirt. I felt I was doing my part for the welfare of my sisters. Father was fully out of control by this time.

"Think you gonna take much of this hot shot?" he asked.

"I can take as much of this as you can dish out," I responded. I knew if I could wear him down or get him so upset and frustrated by not resisting or encouraging the fight, Momma and the girls would be safe that night. He would collapse into an alcohol induced sleep very quickly once he was done. Momma and the girls could return. Father now had something to prove. He wanted to really let me feel the pain of his wrath. He wanted me to cry.

"Want me to stop?" he asked. He started laughing. The ironing cord was now making itself acquainted with my upper torso, lower lumbar area, buttocks, and legs. "Just say out loud you surrender," he said in the most controlled and unemotional tone I heard him speak that night. Each time he snapped the cord, I vowed to hold on for the girls and Momma.

Within a few minutes Father's rage, voice, demeanor, stride, and frustration had collapsed into a whimper and no more rage was evident. Father was completely exhausted. He dropped the cord as he stumbled toward the bedroom door. I moved out of his way and he fell into the room and landed on his bed. He was dead silent. My entire backside seemed numb. I suddenly felt something warm with a salty burn seeping down me. I tried to find solace in the fact it had been my body which was abused instead of the body of my sister or, perhaps Momma. My only thought was to see if Momma had taken the girls to safety.

I started toward the front door. Soreness was already present. My entire back was burning like it had been set afire. Each step I took caused the torn flesh to pull apart. As I stepped down onto the front porch area of our house, the breeze felt somewhat cooling to my backside. Momma came running towards me.

"Are you alright? I should have never left!" she said.

"I'm fine," I responded. Momma put her arms around me to embrace and comfort me. The contact of her hands on my back was more than I could stand. I winced and then pulled back. As Momma quickly pulled her hands away from me, she realized the absolute brutality which had taken place. Momma's hands were covered with blood. She screamed, "What happened?" she asked as she whirled me around. There was a loud gasp from both girls. I turned back to face them. I felt I needed to calm them so not to waken Father.

"It's okay. Just a little accident. I must not have ducked as often as I should have," I said.

"Let me take that shirt off of you and look at your back," Momma commanded. As she removed my tattered shirt, I could feel it tearing away from the quickly dried blood. The coagulation had started the healing process. New fresh blood oozed from the newly formed wounds.

"I think we better get you to a doctor," Momma said.

"No! I'll be OK. It will heal. Can you put some cream or salve on it?" I inquired.

"We don't have much. I'll put on what I have," she said. I looked at Karen and Frances. Karen had stopped crying.

"You girls OK?"

"Yeah," said Frances. Karen was still in shock from the sight of my back.

"Thanks bub. That should have been me. I really am sorry it happened." We all headed back into the house. Momma went to her bedroom door. She stopped before entering. Father was snoring. We could hear him through the closed door.

She went into the room to find some type of medicine for me.

My back was already getting sore. I knew that by tomorrow it would be too sore to go to school. What hurt more was that I knew there would be no way I could run in the track meet scheduled for tomorrow.

"Why did you let him beat you like this?" she asked. "You should have fought back," Momma whispered. This was the first time she had ever uttered those words in the many instances that Father had "punished" any of us. Right then in that second, I vowed to myself it would be the last time anything like that would be tolerated if the punishment was to me or directed to anyone I cared for.

"If it hadn't been me, it would have been one of you. I didn't want my sisters or you to be beaten. He had to take it out on someone so I thought it might as well be me. But I don't know if I will ever be able to let him hit me again Momma. I know Father had a horrible childhood, but that is the last time I will tolerate such abuse," I promised.

"Son, you know he doesn't mean to do this much damage. He just gets carried away. He doesn't know when to stop," Momma was already defending him.

"I used to believe that Momma. I don't anymore. He knows exactly what he is doing all of the time. You can make excuses if you want, but I won't any longer.

I know it is late, but I have to walk over to the coach's house and explain to him that I can't compete tomorrow," I said. Momma looked like I was about to expose something to society which was lethal.

"Son, you gonna tell someone from school your daddy beat you? That will get us all in trouble," she insisted.

"I won't tell him Father beat me OK?" I said as I tried to ease her apprehension. I put on a long-sleeved shirt and made sure not to button or tuck it in my pants. As I walked toward my coach's house, I tried to come up with a believable alibi. Coach lived across town from us, so I had some time to plan my strategy.

As I approached his door, it was quite obvious he was asleep or not at home. It was 11:30 p.m. I was sure he expected all of his athletes to be asleep too. I swallowed hard, stood as straight as possible, and knocked firmly on the door. There was no answer. I knocked again. A light appeared in the window at the south end of the house. Then another light appeared in the living room. The outside light suddenly appeared as bright as a spotlight.

Coach opened the door very cautiously. Once he recognized me, he opened it further. Yawning, he said, "Reel, this better be good. You should be in bed. Don't tell me you can't sleep and just happened to be in the neighborhood. Or maybe you are sleepwalking, just woke up so you decided to drop by!" he said with a smile. I appreciated his light-hearted attempt at humor. He knew I would never just drop by without being invited unless there was an emergency.

"Coach, I need to talk to you for just a couple of minutes," I said looking down and away from him. I didn't want to look directly into his eyes because he could always get any information, he wanted from me.

"Well, would you like to come in, or did you want to talk under the stars?" he said motioning for me to enter. "I always have time for a student who needs me," Coach said with another smile. He propped the door wide open. Then he sat down on his sofa. "Okay, what's up?" He had turned serious.

"I can't go to the meet tomorrow. In fact, I need you to write a pass excusing me from P.E. for the next couple of weeks," I said getting into the formal speech I had prepared on the way to his house. My tone was not quite as strong as I had practiced.

"Wait just a minute. Slow down. What do you mean, you can't run in tomorrow's meet? We have all been practicing really hard for this meet," he said paying special attention to certain words that he chose to stress.

His voice showed him more concerned with the reason why I would be letting the team down than with my not running.

"This isn't your style. I can always depend on you. Something else must have happened. What?" His eyes were searching for mine. I tried to avoid them. He stood up. I felt bad; but I did not want him to inform the police that child abuse was going on in the Reel family.

"Coach, I just can't tell you more. Don't you know if there were any way at all that I could, I would? Trust me. I have a very good reason," I declared. I tried not to reveal any more information. By this time, my back was very sore, and I could feel the stiffness with each movement I made.

"Ron, this won't do. Don't you think I deserve more explanation than what you are saying?" he asked. He was now standing looking directly into my eyes. He put his arms up and began to embrace my shoulders paternalistically. The pain from his fingers touching my shoulders caused me to grimace and jump back.

"What's the matter Ron? I am not going to hurt you," he said gently. "I know sir. But my shoulder and back are really sore. If I tell you the truth, will you promise just to listen and not do anything?" I began to cry.

"Well, I definitely will listen. But I don't know if I can just stand by and do nothing. If you have done anything wrong, we'll have to get it corrected. I will stand by you, regardless of what you have done," he promised. I wanted to tell him the truth. Yet, I still wanted to protect Momma and the girls from Father's anger.

"I'm sure it's not school. It has to be home! Right?" he asked.

"Coach, I can't run tomorrow because Father gave me a whipping this evening," I said. My eyes were now completely full of tears. My nose was runny.

"What did you do? Can I talk to your dad and get you forgiven? Were you grounded? Can we get a pardon?" he wondered. "Maybe I can convince him that your running is part of your school requirement for team sports or a class you have to complete. Perhaps we can trade some extra work next weekend that even I can help you do around the house for letting you run," he suggested. Coach was always willing to go the extra mile for his runners. I knew it was time to confess.

"I'm not grounded. I'll just be too sore to run," I told him.

"Nonsense, we'll put you in the whirlpool, then massage the soreness out. He didn't beat you, did he? You look pretty good to me. Turn around and I will look for gaping and ugly marks on your backside," he said trying to lighten the moment. These words were too close for comfort. I cried as I spoke, "You're wrong, Coach. He did beat me. He cut the cord off the iron and he beat me until he passed out," I said. "What are you talking about? Slip out of your shirt and let me see your back?" he demanded.

"Do you promise you won't do anything? Please! It won't do any good. If they arrest him, he'll just beat us up worse when he gets out. He only does it when he's drunk. Momma's real sick and he can't quite face up to that, Coach." I tried to defend the family to him. Coach was unbuttoning my shirt when he saw my side and back. His temper exploded. "Ron, how could you let him do something like this? Why didn't you defend yourself? Why didn't you run away?" he asked. Coach was headed to his bathroom to get medications.

"I think it's time I go see your father. It's not safe for you to be there. It certainly isn't safe for your sisters or Mom," he said.

"Lie down on the floor on your stomach," he said.

"Coach, please, you promised. If you say or do anything, it will just wind up getting worse," I said. Coach spread some type of gel, which was both soothing and cooling, on my back.

"I can't believe this. You'll be out a few weeks. You won't even be able to move tomorrow. I'm surprised you can walk and move as well as you can right now. Where is your Dad?" he wanted to know.

"He passed out and was asleep when I left. In the morning he'll be surprised when he finds out what he did. He only meant to whip me; he just got carried away," I replied, though I knew that what I was telling him was a lie.

"No one gets this carried away without knowing what he is doing. I don't know what to do, but you are right. You won't be able to run tomorrow." Coach helped me put my shirt back on and offered me a ride home. I told him the brisk air would feel good hitting my back from the loose shirt. As soon as I said the word "hitting" we both looked at each other and felt a very moving and pure connection between us.

"As I started to walk away, Coach called out, "Ron, I'll think of a good reason why you are not at school in the morning. Call me if there is any kind of problem when you get home. I will come right over and get you."

Of course, I never called him back. When I got home, Father, Momma, and the girls were all asleep. We appeared like one big happy family. It was, however, only the quiet before the storm. Little did I know I would never go back to Clovis High School.

CHAPTER EIGHT

When I woke up the next morning, Father had already gone to work. My back was so sore I could hardly move. Many times, earlier in my life my legs had been cut and had bled after I had been disciplined by my father; but this time was different. My entire back was either bruised, or raw. Momma checked on me. She was embarrassed that her husband, my father, had beaten one of his children so severely and that she had done nothing to stop such an attack on her own child.

"You alright?" she asked. The tone of her voice indicated how embarrassed she was at what had taken place. Her hesitancy in seeking to find out exactly how much damage had been done was her attempt to rectify in some fashion the out-of-control behavior her husband had displayed the night before. She had been his victim many times before. Her arm had been broken. Her jaw had been broken. Teeth had been lost. The torture she had experienced at Father's hands was a constant reminder to her how volatile their relationship was.

"Your Dad got up this morning and couldn't remember anything much about last night. You know how he forgets what he does when he wakes up from being so drunk," she claimed.

"What exactly did he remember?" I asked. "I believe that people who drink and blame the alcohol for causing their action simply are not man or woman enough to take responsibility for their own actions. Perhaps alcohol allows the perpetuator of bad behavior to feel empowered enough to perform that specific action; however, it never causes them to do something the person does not want to do."

"He could only remember there was some type of crying that woke him," she said. Momma wanted to try and calm the waters that Father had stirred. She wanted things to return to a moment before this tragedy had taken place.

"He didn't remember beating me until he was so exhausted that he collapsed?"

"No, and I didn't want to stir up anything more, so I just went along with him." This was the same story Momma had told many times before. She had told it so often she almost believed it herself.

"Momma, this has to end. We can't continue to defend his actions. He needs to be responsible for them. I am not going to let him beat any of us again regardless of what I have to do," I said in the most controlled manner I could. I had made up my mind from this time forward his unchecked behavior was going to be exposed to those willing to listen.

"When he sees what he did to you, he will feel awful. He loves you in his own special way," Momma said.

"He has a strange way of showing it. I am going to tell him how I feel tonight," I said.

"That is funny, your dad said he wanted to talk with you tonight when he gets home. He wanted me to make sure you would be here." For the rest of the day, I wondered why he would want to make sure I was home when he returned from the fields.

To this day I cannot explain why Father was always unhappy with me. I thought I was a good child. I was the only son who had never been in any trouble with the police. I never stole, never talked back, never smoked, and never lied. I was desperately trying to live a life that would please God. I stayed home from school. I was planning how and when I would be able to return to school.

Just before Father got home, I said a silent prayer asking for direction and especially for tact in dealing with him because of what had just happened the night before. I heard the front door open and Father came through. You could tell he had experienced a rough day. His clothes were dirty, his face covered with oil and grass, and he had a cut just above his right eye.

"What happened to you?" I asked.

"Just another day in the life of me workin to provide for all of yuns," he said.

"How did you cut your eye?" I wondered.

"The backhoe hit me when I wasn't payin tention. I been thinkin today that me and you need to talk just between us," he said.

"I think that is a good idea."

"Let's go outside so we can talk honestly with each other," he suggested. He opened the front door and headed to the front yard where we had two chairs sitting out near one of the chinaberry trees.

"What in heaven's name you tryin to do boy? You are creating a problem here in this here home."

"I don't know what I have done that is wrong," I replied.

"You are always questioning the decisions your Ma and I make about everything. You talk back about the things we tell you have to be done," he spoke.

"I don't think I talk back. I only question things that could be done differently that would be better for all of us."

"You just gone as far as I'm gonna let ya. None of the older boys ever sassed me. I been tryin to let you slide because your Ma's sick, and she gets upset when I whip ya. But you been havin one big whippin comin a long time," he said.

"Is that why you beat me so hard last night?" I asked. Suddenly he turned his body to face me. He drew his arm back beside his head. I could see the muscles in his arm tight with tension.

"You got what was comin. Why can't you be like all of the other boys? The other boys never stayed in the house cookin, cleanin, carrin on."

"If I don't help Momma with all these chores around the house, how is it going to get done? I realize that you and Donald are closer, and he helped you out in the fields and even worked on the car. But he is not here anymore, he is gone to Aunt Rita and Uncle Pete's," I said trying to clarify my position.

"Boy, don't start. You always could of gone out in the fields at night with me...or worked on the car and stuff with me; but you didn't," he said.

"I'm not saying I couldn't have; but I didn't want to! I don't like to do that stuff. When I graduate from college, I am going to pay someone else to change the oil in my car. I don't want to pick grapes, or potatoes, or oranges. I want to make enough money to pay someone to do that kind of work. But, let me ask you this question, why didn't you come to see me in any of my plays, or when I sing, or when I am in a speech contest? Why don't you care about me?" I asked.

"Listen here boy. I ain't gonna get up in front of all them rich friends from church or school of yours and bow and say how wonderful it is to see em and try to fit in and be funny just cause of you. I don't got the same kinds of clothes or cars, or anything else as them." He was starting to shout.

"I don't expect you to put on a show for them. They accept me as I am. They will accept you. I am not ashamed of my family. I am proud of us. Do you know what I feel like when I'm the only student in any type of competition at school without a parent to watch? I feel like a little puppy dog not good enough for anyone to claim. Just once I wanted to look out from the stage or look to the grandstands and see you and Momma sitting there watching me. But you never come. Are you ashamed of me?" I asked. With that question, he sneered and made no effort to restrain a chuckle.

"Well, you're silly, just like your Ma."

When I heard this statement, I responded without thinking how cruel he could be at certain times.

"Well, then, why did you have me if I'm so silly?" I asked. He clenched his fist and pointed his finger directly into my face. They were deliberate, calculated, and swift as a two-edged sword.

"You really want to know that?" he asked.

"Yeah, I want to know."

"You promise never to tell yar Ma what I'm gonna tell ya?" he asked with a smirk on his face.

"Sure, it's just between us."

"Son, I never thought about having you. You weren't ever considered. All I was doin was having fun for myself with your Ma; you were simply the result of me havin some fun. In fact, I am sorry I had you," he declared.

I was devastated. "I am sorry your fun turned out to be so bad and rotten for you," I said. I wanted so desperately to hear him say that I was not rotten, but good. I wanted him to say I was not a mistake. I wanted him to say we could fix this out-of-control conversation. Yet, his manhood was threatened, and he would not alter the course he had chosen.

"You know what they say, 'Gotta have some bad with the good.' If it hadn't been for you and the other kids still at home, I could be gone and have my freedom from all this," he said.

I didn't want to hear that I had not been wanted. I didn't need the knowledge I was responsible for blocking Father's path to happiness. "I'm sorry I was born to you. I'm sorry you think you have to stay here because of me. I guess I could go live with one of the older kids if that would make you feel better," I said.

"Do what? Don't make no difference to me if you leave," he said.

"Do you want me to go?" I asked again.

"I don't really care where ya go or what ya do. You better know that I ain't got no money to send ya some place and then go and getcha back here. I can't pay somebody to keep ya either."

"I have had a job ever since I can remember. I won't need your money. I have enough money to catch the bus to wherever I go. Will you at least take me to the bus?" I asked. I couldn't understand why he didn't see this had gone too far. Why couldn't he see I was needed here at home during this very tense and terrifying time for all of us. Why couldn't he tell me I was needed.

"I'll gladly take ya," he said. I turned and walked back into the house. Momma had heard us arguing.

"Are you OK?" she asked.

"Yes, I'm fine Momma," I replied. She knew something was wrong. I sat down beside her and took her hand.

"Momma, I can't continue living here at home. Father and I are fighting all the time. This kind of chaos isn't good for you. I need to go away for a little while. As soon as some of the tension ends, I'll come back."

"Where are you gonna go? What you gonna do?" she asked because she wanted to know that I would be safe. I could see tears beginning to form in her eyes.

"I will call my brother Paul and his wife and ask them if I can come and stay with them for a little while," I replied.

"But what about your high school, your job, your church, the cosmetology school on Saturdays? You gonna just give those things up?"

"Momma, it's hard for me too. I don't know all of the answers right now. I won't give them up, but they'll have to wait. I can't go on fighting Father. I just can't," I said.

"Maybe Father will be in a better mood once I am gone. It will be one less headache he will have; one less mouth to feed. I am going to leave my Chevy, which Raymond help me get last summer to use at college, here with you so you can have transportation when you need it." I gave her the keys to my car. "I have enough money to go wherever I need to on the bus and I'll get a job as soon as I get there to help them. I will write every single day. I will do my best to come and see you at Christmas. Whatever happens, you're going to get well and one day I'll be able to take care of you the way you deserve," I promised. By this time Father was standing impatiently waiting. He had cleaned up and was ready to go.

"Bill, don't you think he should stay?" asked Momma.

"Wasn't my idea; was his," he said. I put all of my clothes in a big brown paper bag. I walked over and kissed Momma. I told her goodbye. My parents did not say another word. I walked out of the house feeling orphaned.

When I got to the bus stop, I called my eldest brother Brandon and his wife, who lived in Downey, California, but they did not answer. I called Hannah and Jasper who were in the military about to move to Germany, but they did not answer. Finally, Paul and his wife who lived in Northern California in Antioch answered. This town was about ten miles from where my twin Donald was living with Aunt Rita and Uncle Pete. I asked Paul if I could come to live with them for a few months. He and his wife gave me permission. So, I got on the bus that arrived about two hours after Father dropped me off. I knew I had to be careful the next couple of weeks about moving too quickly or turning directions until my back healed more. Ten hours later I arrived in Antioch.

Paul and his wife met me at the bus station. On the drive to their house, they informed me I would have to get a job to help with expenses. By the end of the first week of my moving to Antioch, I had landed a job in a grocery store and was helping to support myself. I didn't want to be a burden on them. They had three children ages three, six, and seven at home. The store manager hired me to work twenty-five hours per week. I worked after school or in the evenings during school days and on Saturday and Sunday. I agreed to give them fifty percent of my check each pay period to offset my living with them. I waited one week to enroll at the school. My back had not yet mended completely.

I only needed three classes to complete what was required for graduation, so I was able to select three electives. In addition to those required classes, I selected choir, speech, and typing. These three classes had some of the most popular, smartest, and friendliest students at Thomas Jefferson High School. I made several friends the first couple of days in school. They were involved in most of the clubs on campus. They got me to join speech, choir, yearbook, drama, and one club I had never heard of which was called "School Spirit" where you attended any and all extracurricular activities, cheering and supporting the school teams.

My organizational skills were tested early and often that semester. I had to fit everything into my work schedule which often made me late for many of the outside activities. My new friends always accepted me once I arrived because they knew I was really working and not making excuses for not showing up on time.

It was almost two weeks to the date of my arrival, when I had to go to my first PE class at the school. I had avoided this class for a week because I did not have the proper clothing to dress for PE. I quickly found out the PE class I was assigned was a running class. This class was tasked with teaching students how to run the one mile race. I found out our

PE class had been preparing to see how many students could run the mile around or slightly over five minutes. A five-minute mile time would get you noticed at most running meets, but that time was about twenty seconds off the elite time needed for state final placing. I felt like this was a class made for me.

For several weeks the PE teacher had us running laps, but without times being called out or even logged; so, no one would know if any improvement was taking place. This did not make sense to me. Some of the boys were pretty good. Most, however, did not take our goal seriously. The top four guys were going to be selected to be on the mile relay team for the spring semester. I thought I could run at least a time of four minutes and forty seconds on a good day. I knew, however, I had more than a fifty percent chance of not being in Antioch after the semester ended.

As the date approached for us to be tested, I could easily tell the four fastest runners. I knew this because we had begun running by ourselves early in the mornings before school. We were meeting at 6:00 a.m. each day to run. My group of five, as I called us, were encouraging me to run as part of the group. I started to help coach our group. When we were practicing before school, I sometimes ran faster than they could run. They were pleasantly surprised. I had just arrived at the school. They had been practicing since June.

I told them about our track and cross-country team at Clovis and the incredible coach we had. I told them I was only as good I was because we were forced to run each day against him and were pushed each day to be better than the day before. I challenged them to try to stay up with me the best they could. I tried to coach as I had been coached. I also shared with them that I was not going to run faster than they when we were tested because I wanted them to be rewarded for their work and dedication. I also revealed that I probably would not return after Christmas.

On the day the entire class was to run to see who the top runners were, our PE teacher made an announcement I had not seen coming. None of us knew he had been watching us do our special morning workouts. He had even called my old coach and asked about me and my best times. He said to us, "This is the day we have been working toward. Today we will be deciding on our mile relay team for next semester. We are seeking five runners today not four. I have found out that Ron has the potential to become one of the top mile runners in the state. We need to find three or four other people that can help him gain some notoriety for us. Ron, I am expecting you to set a new school record for us today. We have never had a runner go below five minutes."

I did not know what to say or do. I turned to my group. I was caught in a situation I did not want. I no longer had a desire to run for competition. I replied, "I don't want to disappoint you but that was then. I have not been working out at such a high level for some time. I have been hurt lately and don't think you should have such a high expectation of me. I always start out fast, but I can't maintain that speed for the entire mile."

They looked at me and all said, "Do your best." "Try your hardest." "Go for it." "Give it your all." I wanted to belong to this group. I did not want there to be a them and a me.

I called back to them, "Run the race of your life today!"

The gun sounded and we were off. The five of us were out front before the first lap ended. By the beginning of the third lap, we were almost two thirds a lap ahead of some of the other runners. Some had given up. My teammates were encouraging me to run my best. I started to accelerate. As I started to move out faster, they found a new level and were not far behind me. We were now starting the final lap. There were only five us still running. All the other runners had given up and were on the sidelines cheering us on. I eased up just a bit. I was so impressed with the other four. We were now on the back side of the track. We would soon be headed home. I could feel the distance between me and them shortening. I adjusted my speed down slightly. We were about one hundred yards from the finish. I knew how much this meant to them.

Many races have what is called the rabbit. That person is supposed to get out in front of the group and set a pace that makes the others run fast, but that person cannot sustain that speed for the entire race. They will drop out of the race when their job is completed. I felt my job had been completed. I ran to the grass and got off the track. The four boys in my practice group all continued to run to the finish line. Three of them ran slightly over the five-minute time. The other hit five minutes exactly. They were the new heroes for the school.

From the time I arrived in Antioch, I knew my academic goal was to finish the six classes I was taking that semester so I would only need one class next semester to graduate. I had to be ready to return to the Fresno area if needed. I decided to start picking up some additional work on the weekends when I did not have shifts at the store.

One Sunday afternoon when I was weeding in an almond field, I had a visitor. I had just stopped for lunch and was sitting under one of the trees eating a sandwich when a new station wagon slowly pulled up. At first, I thought it might be the owner. My brother, Paul, had gotten me the job and I had not met the owner. As the car came closer, I saw it was Donald. I had not seen him since I arrived. He was not attending my high school. When I phoned him, he said he was busy and would get with me when he had a chance. He stopped right in front of where I was sitting. He got out of the car and spoke, "What you think about my ride? They call me Cool Breeze. Aunt Rita and Uncle Pete have three cars and I can choose any of them to drive. Man, I got it made. Sorry I didn't come to see you sooner, but I don't want them to know you are up here too. They might want to adopt you too. That would not work out for me," he said with a smile on his face. "Really, it's a shame you have to work like this on Sunday. But, better you than me. I got to get home cause it is almost lunch time."

I said to him, "I thought you were going to high school here. I never see you at any school function. I have asked around about you and none of the students seem to know you."

Donald smiled and then spoke, "I go by their last name. I am Donald Nelson now. They want to adopt me. I cannot let them down, so I agreed to be their son. We tried home-schooling, but that didn't work out. I am going into the Army in January."

I must have looked dumbfounded. Since I knew he was only seventeen, I asked, "How is that possible? You are only seventeen. We won't be eighteen until June." Donald waved me off as he turned and headed toward his car.

"Granny went and told them I did not have a birth certificate. She signed a document that I was eighteen. Don't go and mess things up." He started his car and left. I did not have a personal conversation with him again until he had been in the military for three years. When he was told he was going to be sent to Vietnam, he phoned me and wanted to know if I would join the Army and volunteer to go to Vietnam because they would not send both twins there at the same time. I did not volunteer.

By Christmas, I had saved enough money to buy presents for Momma, Father, Karen, and Frances. I took the bus back to visit my family. The bus pulled into Fresno early in the morning. Pastor DeWolfe picked me up at the bus station. We went back to his home in Clovis. I waited until that night to go home. I wanted everyone to be there. Pastor dropped me off at the house that evening. Once I arrived in front of their house, I walked eagerly toward what used to be my home. I knocked on the door and Karen answered.

"Oh! Oh! Momma! Frances! Look, Brother is home!" she screamed. A quick glance showed me that Momma's condition had worsened. She had continued to lose weight. It turned out that in the nine weeks I had been gone, she had lost over forty pounds. I knew she needed me at home.

"Son, you've come home for Christmas, huh?" she asked.

"No Momma, I've come home for good. I'll call and get my classes transferred and give notice at the store. I'm going to stay home if Father will let me," I replied.

I asked Father for permission to return. His reply was simply stated before the whole family, "I never said you had to go," he said as he sighed with relief.

I could tell he was tired of trying to hold the family together. I had to go back to Antioch the week after Christmas to take my final exams. Because of the extra classes I had taken during the fall semester, I only needed one class to graduate from high school. Once I got back to Clovis, Momma gave me back the keys to my car, and I immediately enrolled at Fresno Adult High School for an evening class. I reenrolled as a full-time student at the Cosmetology College. This was a forty-hour weekly commitment so I could graduate and take my statewide licensing exam by mid-July. My adult class met one night per week. By attending these schools, I would have the opportunity to enroll at Trinity University in the fall of 1968.

CHAPTER NINE

An exploratory surgery on Momma in December 1967, revealed that, in addition to hepatitis, she had pancreatic cancer, which had spread throughout her body. The doctors at St. Luke's Hospital gave her six months to live. At Momma's insistence, we decided not to tell my younger sisters, Karen and Frances. I don't think you can really hide something so important from those affected by it; they will find out eventually, but Momma said she did not want them to worry about her. The doctors told us she could come home for now; in a few months, however, they said the pain would become so bad she would have to return to the hospital. On April 15, 1968, we took Momma back to St. Luke's Hospital, where she spent the last days of her life.

As Momma continued to weaken physically, she tried very hard not to show it to her children. She would always tell the two youngest girls she was feeling better and would be home soon. I knew differently and they sensed it too. The hospital room looked so dreary. The pale walls and worn flooring blended together in a dismal way; they provided a perfect setting for illness and death. Momma's complexion was very pale. Her hair was uncombed. It had been nine weeks since the last time she had been strong enough for me to brush and color her hair. Something had to be done. I closed the door and in the next hour a hair color transformation took place. It was about 9:30 p.m. when I finished. None of the other children had come to the hospital that day. Father, as usual, had failed to come to visit. Momma began a conversation I had been dreading.

"Son, where do you think your father was tonight?" she asked. I thought quickly. I knew Father had either been out drinking or he had been out with another woman, or both. I lied to her.

"Oh, he probably had to work late. He's been asking for more hours to help us with the extra gas we need to drive into Fresno all the time. He says he hates it when he can't get here; but you know him, he says he can't just shake a tree for the money we need." I said a quick prayer asking forgiveness for lying to her and continued to look into Momma's eyes hoping she would not see through my performance. She was in so much pain. Her eyes were glassy.

"Do you think your dad loves me?" she asked.

"Momma, that's a silly question. Look at all the years you and Father have been together. Two people who don't love each other don't stay together and have ten children." I wanted to change the subject. I did not want to express my true feelings about Father.

"Do you think I've been a good mother?" she asked. I felt a knot form right in the middle of my throat. On some levels no child could have asked for a better parent. She always wanted the best for her children. Her decision to allow Father to avoid responsibility for his actions, from drinking to the physical abuse to her and their children, was problematic; but, at the same time, understandable. He had been her husband since she was a teen. He was the only man with whom she had sexual relations.

She knew in her heart what he did when he drank was wrong, but she tried to ignore it.

"Momma, you have been the best mother a child could ever want," I replied.

"Do you really think that? We didn't have much to give you kids. You had hand-me-down clothes, we had secondhand furniture, used appliances..." she would have continued; but I interrupted,

"We had plenty; and then some." I continued to hide my feelings in an attempt to lessen her insecurity and to try to divert her attention to a different subject matter.

"A very wise woman once told me money doesn't buy love. Respect does that!" I said, quoting what she had once said to me. Her eyes were now full of tears. She knew the end was coming soon. She wanted to be free of the secret she had held for many years.

"Momma don't cry. You'll get me crying. I'm almost a grown man. I don't think that would look good at this time," I whispered. Her face was intent. She had mustered enough energy to partially sit up in her bed. It was time for her to try to comfort me and lay to rest any insecurities she thought I had about myself. I had been ill most of my life from two bouts of rheumatic fever, tonsillitis, breast cancer, anemia, heart murmur, and gingivitis so severe I had undergone several oral surgeries.

"I know the pain and sorrow you have felt growing up. You didn't ever talk about it; but son, I've known it and it has bothered you a lot. You've been different from your twin and we've made a big deal, well, your Dad has made it into an issue, but you need to know he loves you in his own special way," she asserted. "Your dad can't express himself very good. He can't be emotional. I think that has been the biggest difference between the two of you. You're soft and tender but assertive when you need to be, and your dad is threatened by that. But you need to know he has always been proud of you. You are the one he knows will make something of yourself," she said. As I heard this statement, I felt safe enough to ask the question that had plagued me every time I participated in any social event where I felt alone.

"If the two of you were so proud of me, why didn't either of you come to anything I ever did at school? I was always the only kid without an adult at those functions," I recalled. Momma thought for a minute before answering. I could tell she was trying to make sure she answered the question truthfully but delicately.

"I think you're old enough and mature enough to understand what I am going to say. We've always been poor, all our lives. I let myself go without, so I could give you kids a little more. Now, I never told you this before, but I...we never went many places in public because we didn't want to embarrass you," she said. For just a moment, I didn't know if I had actually heard what she had stated. How does a parent think she could possibly embarrass her child by attending a school or church event to watch a performance as an audience member?

"How could you embarrass me Momma?" I asked. I really needed some clarification.

"I didn't have any decent shoes or a nice dress, or..." she was telling me. For the first time in my life, I understood her feeling of embarrassment. Her pain could be felt when I heard her say the words, "decent shoes" and "nice dress."

"You dressed fine for me. You always looked good to me," I said. Not once had I ever thought either of my parents dressed in an unacceptable manner. All of our clothes were always clean and pressed.

"I had those missing teeth; I looked ugly," she added. Suddenly I remembered that one Friday evening when I was in sixth grade and I brought over a new friend, Bobby Jones, to ask permission to visit him across town. He was the son of Dr. Jones and I had first met him when I had been hospitalized for two weeks with tonsillitis and his father had brought him along on his rounds. Now we were in the same grade and classroom. Bobby had told me when I returned to school, he would like to hang out more often. They lived on the other side of town, so we had walked six blocks from school to ask if I could go to his house for a birthday party his parents were throwing for him.

When we arrived at my house, I could hear screaming and thrown objects hitting walls inside our home. I told Bobby he needed to go home without me, and I would see him on Monday. I explained to him a crisis was taking place and I could not enter the house at that time to seek the permission I needed. He left, and about ten minutes later Father came out the front door, got into his car, and drove away. When I went into the house, Momma was sitting at the kitchen table crying and holding several teeth in her hand. Her mouth was bleeding. Her story was she had slipped on some ice on the kitchen floor. I knew that was not the truth. He had broken her teeth when his fist hit her mouth. Eventually, she had her top teeth pulled and dentures replaced the missing teeth.

"That is not true Momma. I think you're beautiful," I protested.

"Momma forgive me," I added.

"Me forgive you? What have you done?" she asked.

"I always thought you didn't come because you weren't proud of me. Now I know that you stayed away because you thought you would embarrass me," I said. I leaned over the bed and I kissed her on her cheek. Finally, the truth was out. Both of our insecurities were brought into the light.

"Baby, I'm so proud of you," she said.

"I'm so sorry. I never examined the situation from your viewpoint. I was too wrapped up in myself. Sometimes I feel I am mature and other times I feel I am very young and inexperienced in making decisions especially about relationships," I admitted.

"We all feel that way from time to time. People are not perfect. We can't always make wise and mature decisions because if we did, there wouldn't be any way for us to learn from our mistakes. We all make our share of mistakes. We all must learn how to forgive. Always treat the person you are close to with the same care and honesty you want them to give you," she said.

I started to tell her about the time I had run into the kitchen when I was about five or six years old and saw her and Father hugging and kissing one another. I had never seen the two of them displaying any physical touching before then. Having six older brothers and sisters, who were married and were having children of their own, I had noticed that they were always kissing each other when they visited us. Soon after, they would announce they were going to have a baby. I thought that if a boy kissed a girl and she liked it, soon they would have a baby. I thought Momma would enjoy this story, but she had fallen asleep. Her medication had taken effect. She would sleep through the night. At least for a time she would not feel the cancerous cells consuming her body. I scooted my chair to the left side of her bed. I placed my head to rest near her side. I took her hand in mine. I too fell asleep.

Momma had not gone to sleep; she had slipped into a coma. It was difficult to come to the hospital and not have Momma respond to any type of stimuli. The doctors informed us that she could not respond to us, however, there was a chance she could hear us in her present coma condition. They told us there was nothing anyone could do, but to simply watch over her as she continued to deteriorate each day. I continued to talk to her as though she could hear and was simply waiting for her to respond. I would tell her how Father had come to visit her but that she had been asleep. I thought God would forgive me for the white lies I told to make her feel better.

"Momma, the doctors say you can't hear, or feel, or express your thoughts. I'm not saying they are wrong, but sometimes they don't know it all. Your children, I mean your family, sure love you. Your children keep taking turns coming up to visit you. They miss you. They miss hearing you talk to them! Momma, Father misses you too! Perhaps he misses you more than we kids do. He misses you as a wife, as a mother to your children, and as his friend. Father just left a few minutes ago. He had to go home to make sure someone is taking care of the girls. He is working extra hours. He doesn't sleep very well anymore. But you know what Momma? Father kissed you right before he left. He wishes you'd get well soon because he loves you. He told me to make sure I told you just how much he loves you. Momma, he says you are the only woman in the world that he ever loved and, he says that you don't need to worry about him because he's strong and healthy and is managing just fine until you get well so you can be the wonderful wife to him again like you have always been."

That is what I told Momma night after night. In reality, Father was in a bar someplace with another woman. Father had become an alcoholic, and during the daytime he worked on the ranch, and in the evening, he went out to the bars.

I had been keeping a pretty tight schedule of working, going to cosmetology college, night school, church, and staying at the hospital. My body had developed an endurance level and warning system. My limit was three days of non-sleep. I would stay with Momma at night for three consecutive nights. I slept at home on the fourth night. My body would just give out if I pushed it longer than four days.

In one of my rare nights sleeping at home, I was awakened by the cries of my two younger sisters. It was about 1:30 in the morning and they were afraid because Father was not home. This missing parent syndrome had become his usual pattern for the past six months. I tried to comfort them from my bed.

"Girls...Karen, Frances, it's going to be O.K. Father can take care of himself. He's a grown man and he knows what he's doing. Now, go back to sleep," I said. Just as I closed my eyes once again, I heard more sobs and cries coming from their room. Karen was trying to comfort Frances.

"Sissy, he is O.K. You know he is able to take care of himself," she reminded her.

"But what happens if he runs into something or someone and gets hurt or gets killed? Then what are we gonna do? Who'll take care of us then?" Frances asked. I realized I could not help the girls by staying in bed so I got up and went to sit beside them to see if my presence would help.

"Can I help?" I asked.

"Do you really want to?" asked Karen. Her tone had a sharp note to it. The words were clothed with suppressed hurt and sorrow for both Momma and for herself. It sounded like previously bottled-up fear and frustration were suddenly emerging from a once secure child.

"Of course! I know this is rough on the two of you, but it's rough on all of us too...especially..." but before I could continue, Karen joined the conversation:

"Yeah, well where were you when we needed you? You simply left when it got bad for you! We've had to stay here. We've heard it all. We didn't have a place to run to! We were too little. Now we're not supposed to know what's going on. We're told everything is getting better. What do you guys think we are? Stupid? While you were gone and before Momma went to the hospital, we heard them fighting every night. Momma screaming and crying! Daddy hitting and fighting! He jumps on us for everything; even if we haven't done anything," she complained. I knew I had to bring some type of comfort to both of them. I had greatly underestimated how much they knew and how much pain they were experiencing.

"It doesn't matter to you because you are older," Karen continued. "You can just leave again. You're not here at night by yourself wondering if tomorrow you will wake up to not having Momma or Daddy. What's going to happen to us? Where are we going to go? Are we going to have to stay with Daddy? He's out all the time. Are we going to have to leave our friends? Are we going to live with one of the married older kids, not because they want us, but because they feel obligated to finish raising us? We might be younger, but we hurt just as much as you older kids. Our Momma is dying too!"

"You know what, Karen? I guess I have been pretty concerned about myself. I'm sorry. Karen, you're right. Maybe I shouldn't have walked out on the family. I'm trying to make up for it. None of us knows what is going to happen. It's rough on you both, I know. But, right now the best thing you can do is to try not to worry. It's not our place to worry about what is going to happen in the future. That's all going to take care of itself. If we knew what was going to take place in the future, we wouldn't ever get up and try to do our best," I said. I thought if I could take their minds off the immediate situation; it would give them some small amount of emotional relief.

"Remember what we learned in our Sunday school classes? God tells us He won't put anything on us that we can't bear if we trust in Him. We have to believe that statement. It's hard now, but things will get better. You are right. Momma is dying and unless God performs a miracle, she won't be here much longer physically; but she'll be with us in spirit for the rest of our lives. She wants us to continue living. I know Father's not helping matters, but he's going through some difficult things himself." I said this in as comforting a way as possible, considering all that was happening to us.

"Now listen here. I'll put my clothes on and go get Father. Will that make you feel better? I'll find him and I'll bring him home. O.K.?" As I dressed, the crying began to subside. The fact I was going to go find

Father comforted Karen and Frances enough to allow them to return to sleep. I stayed in their room long enough to verify they had both fallen asleep before I left the house.

I learned something very special that night. Just because brothers or sisters are younger does not mean their feelings are less real or less important than those of others. None of us thought a twelve- and fifteen-year-old could know much about what was happening around them, but my sisters knew and understood all of the implications of what could happen to them when Momma passed away.

I was old enough to control my own destiny. They would have to rely on someone to house and protect them. Small children must feel they are loved, needed, secure, and wanted if they are to pay forward such emotions to their own loved ones.

My search for Father started with my asking myself, "Where would I go if I didn't want anyone to find me?" The answer was simple. Los Angeles. Father, however, would not drive to Los Angeles because it was too far away. His car would not make such a lengthy trip. We had never travelled more than an hour on any trip because of the fear our automobile would break down and we couldn't get home. Using Father's logic of where to go and his history of past disappearances, I knew I would find him within a radius of seven to ten miles from Clovis.

Father's car was parked outside a beer joint called the Blue Moon. It was a very scummy looking building and loud western music could be heard in the street. I knew from previous experience that rescuing Father from such a place was not going to be easy. Father would fight hard to stay; he was in his element.

The flashing light rays from the Blue Moon sign shed tainted light onto the situation at hand. Father would fight hard to come up with an excuse for his evening's actions. I despised being in a place like this establishment, but I despised even more, that Father was sitting there partaking of such offerings. The Blue Moon looked no better on the inside than it had from the outside. Most of the customers appeared to be in their late forties or early fifties, the majority of them smoking, and all of them drinking.

There he was, sitting at the corner of the bar. He was snuggled up and embracing a woman with unkempt hair and a cigarette in her hand. She was coaxing him, "Come on Bill. Let's buy me something else to drink. I'll pay for it. You jest give me the money." All of the nights when he returned empty-handed, though he had been paid earlier in the day suddenly made sense. He had not lost the money the way he told us he had. As I walked closer, I saw Father wrapping his hands around the woman trying to steal a kiss. The woman was expertly dodging and teasing him. She was still asking for drink money.

"Father," I said. "I think it is time that we go home."

"Can't ya see I am busy? I'll be home later," he replied.

"I think it's time you come home now and not later. It's already late. I'll help you. We can come back and get your car in the morning. Come on. You need to go with me," I said. I put one arm out to get hold of his shoulder when he pushed me away. The woman responded quickly to my intrusion into her potential business deal.

"Don't you think Billy is capable of deciding who he wants to be with, and where he wants to go, and who he wants to go with?" said the lady at the bar.

"Look, I don't want to start an argument. It's late and time to go home," I insisted.

"Look cutie! I think you better go on home and get out of here because I don't think you look old enough to be in here with the grown men," advised the Blue Moon Lady.

"Ma'am, I would prefer you stay out of this because it really isn't any of your business," I said. I moved closer to reach for Father.

"Ronald, you gettin smart with my friend here?" he asked. I could see and hear his temper about to explode. After many years of observing friends, siblings, and parents, you get to know their verbal and non-verbal intensifying mannerisms.

"I don't think she is your friend, and no, sir, I am not getting smart. Your family is at home worried about you. The girls are crying because they think something might happen to you," I told him. He pushed himself away from the woman and tried to step toward me. It was evident why the two were embraced at the corner of the bar. It was a support for both of their intoxicated bodies. They both lost their balance and I tried to keep them both from falling. I was able to catch Father, but Blue Moon Lady fell from her barstool and landed on the floor. I offered my hand to help her up; but she refused it saying, "Well, what are you goin to do Billy? You gonna go with him or stay here with me?" she asked. I positioned myself so I could begin to push Father toward the door.

"He's coming with me," I insisted. I grabbed hold of Father like he was a one hundred-and-sixty-pound bag of potatoes and we started for the door. He suddenly relaxed and stopped pulling away from me.

"Hey, Babe, I got to go with my kid here. He'll see that I get home. You be here later on durin the week. I'll be back, O.K.?" Once we got outside Father's speech became extremely slurred. He began his alcoholic stupor routine. The following morning it would be the same old story. He couldn't remember what he did, why he did it, or with whom he did it.

"Father, please come with me. We have to get home. You need sleep; the girls need sleep; and I need sleep," I said. I put him in the car, and we started home.

He did not say anything to me. I tried to coax him into discussing our family problem.

"I don't understand why you feel the urge to go out night after night like this. I'm sure the pressure on you now is more than on anyone else. Father, you have always been strong. We need you to continue to be strong," I said. I wanted him to see that, in my own way, I recognized his vulnerability. His world was so different now. He drank to distract himself from having to deal with the impending death of his wife, the planning of what to do with the children at home, and what he was willing to do to help himself out of a great depression.

"Ronald, you know I only do this cause I'm a man right? I got these urges inside and they just happin. I mean, your Momma is up there in the hospital and when I go to a place like the Blue Moon, those women like me. They find me sexy," he said almost under his breath.

"Your sexual urges and drives aren't the only things in your world that needs your attention right now," I said.

"I knowed ya couldn't understand cause you ain't married. You still a little virgin. A man's urge is stronger than for a woman," he said.

"The urge we need you to face right now is survival. We need you. Those two little girls at home need you. Just before I left, they were crying their hearts out. Every night you go out and do this bar scene you make them more and more frightened. When you are not at home, they fantasize about where you are, whether or not you will get in a wreck, whether or not you will come home, if you are going to wind up in the hospital, or worse yet if you have died. Finally, in their minds, they wonder if they will lose both parents. All they know for sure is that you are not home where a parent should be in this situation," I said.

"Sonny, don't tell me ya worried about your old pappy here. I been takin care of myself since I was a little boy," he bragged.

"I know, but we don't need you to act like this. We tell Momma every night you have been by to see her, but that she was asleep and missed you. Don't you think she knows you're not there? You're going to have to put these feelings you are having away until the end; at least until after Momma dies," I said, trying hard not to cry.

These words had no effect on my passenger. Father had passed out and would say in the morning he could not remember any of our conversation. The only solace to be found in this drinking episode was that for at least one more night, Father was safe.

When we got home, I helped him get into his bed. He had just enough strength to get from the car to his bed where he seemed to fall immediately to sleep. I, for one, thought it was all a game of deceit. He did not have to talk about what had happened. He did not want to talk about having left my sisters on their own. He did not want to think about what life would be like without Momma. He wanted to pretend that everything was still under his control. He was mistaken.

CHAPTER TEN

While Father was safe at home, Momma was continually getting weaker each day. It was almost June. I looked forward to June 6, 1968. On that day, I would graduate from high school. I would have only two weeks afterwards before I would take the state exam for becoming a professional cosmetologist.

I had officially completed my required hours and floor time so that the cosmetology school would certify me eligible for the state examination. The college gave those of us who had finished the course work what they called "Baby" State Board Exams. This was an attempt to create a close approximation of all the conditions in the practical portion of the test as well as a chance to practice for the written examinations. I had passed our school's written examinations with 100% accuracy. I had been asked to help some of the other not-so-academic students prepare for this part. The practical portion of the examination was considered the hardest by many. If you did one thing wrong in the application of a towel around the neck, over direction of a roller, too large a section for a haircut application, or over depositing of hair color or bleach for the hair coloring segment, you would be told to begin again.

The annual statewide hair competition would take place in three weeks. Each cosmetology school in the Fresno County area sent students to compete for the right to represent our county at the State Finals Student Competition. The Fresno competition had forty-five students competing for the right to represent their school at the state finals in four categories. My beauty college had eight contestants. Our college had never qualified more than two students to the state finals.

The Fresno area could send three students in each competitive category to the Biltmore Hotel in Los Angeles to represent the county. This year the contest would be held at our school with students competing in four categories, cutting, coloring, formal look, and fantasy creations. I knew a student, Shawnda, at one of the other colleges through a friend of mine in Clovis and she wanted to go to Los Angeles, but she wanted to go as a model and not as a competitor. She begged me to use her as my model for the completion. I agreed.

The night before the competition, we met and I created a short cut on the sides that I fashioned into outstanding finger waves flowing effortlessly into the back section where I directed the hair up four inches higher than her head by creating actual finger curls directing the hair first in an upwards direction, then feathering the top like you would in either a beehive or French twist look. I created an inverted up-twist back that blended into the side and from the front looked like a flip on one side. I then teased the front section into a higher portion of hair and created what I called tear drop curls smoothly blending into the top of the back movement.

We had bleached her hair platinum and I had chosen a color called "Wedding White" for the blonde color. Once I had the hairstyle set, dried, and combed, I took three different sized brushes and three different shades of brown, and outlined (created) painted movement transitioning into the completed coiffed product. Shawnda then slipped into a formal dress, high heels, and fake pearls to accent the brown and platinum hair and her very dark sun-tanned body. She was a swimmer.

That Saturday competition produced a result that amazed this contestant, onlookers, judges, and models. Our college thought the two women who had been doing hair for over twenty years and finally decided to get licensed would win in the hair cutting and coloring divisions.

What they did not expect, however, was for me to be any competition to them or anyone else. The judges revealed the top three in each category. My model was called forward in the cutting, color, and formal categories. Shawnda and I were the only team that had been recognized in more than one category. The rules stated that if you were one of the top three in more than one category, you had to choose one category for the state competition. Sarah and Darlene placed in the top in one category each. We placed in the top three in all three categories.

I chose to advance to the state finals in the formal category so as not to be in competition with contestants from my own school. It was the first time three students had ever advanced to the state finals from the same cosmetology college. Although Sarah and Darlene never thanked me for not advancing in the same category where they had placed, I knew that by this time, neither wanted me as their competition. Hard work and practice finally brought me an award and respect. I was very proud of this honor.

We went to the finals in Los Angeles. This was my first trip south over the "grape-vine" as that part of CA 99 is called. I never had seen so many cars, houses, hotels, and people. When we got to the Biltmore Hotel where the competition was being held, I was in awe of the beauty of the building, the rooms where we styled our models, and the other competitors.

The category in which Fresno was not represented was Fantasy. I saw hair displayed in a number of ways I had never imagined possible. Hair was different colors, lengths, and even used for costumes. One model had nothing over her body but hair. As I reflect now as a mature adult, it may have been my nerves, the trash talking by some of my competitors, my lack of confidence, superior talent on the part of my opponents, or all of these together that caused me not to advance to the final round of competition. I was disappointed, but I still had a lot on my plate.

I could not wait for the next three weeks to end. Then I would be able to slow down a little. The older children did their best to drop by the hospital whenever possible. The last days of the month were days of strain and worry for all. As a Christian, I wanted to make sure Momma had accepted her savior before her death. She had accepted Him. I was fortunate enough to pray with her when she professed her belief in Him.

She said, "Ronald, do you remember when you twins graduated from the eighth grade?"

"Sure. I remember. We were living in Fowler in those two little houses. It was a proud day for both of us. You had suffered a heart attack and we were afraid you wouldn't be able to attend," I said. I had not thought about that graduation for almost four years.

"Remember what I told you?" she asked. I couldn't ever forget it.

"I told you I wanted you to graduate not only from eighth grade, but from high school. I want you to graduate this year too," she said. I was not sure where she was going with this conversation.

"I will graduate. I have only a couple of weeks left. I will be your first son to graduate from high school," I said. Just as I was telling her this, she fell back on the pillow. With all the control of her body she could muster, she brought her head back up and said, "The same thing applies now. I want you to graduate from high school now and college too! These two graduations will be just for me. I might not be there. If I'm not there in body, I will be there in spirit," she said. Those were the last words I remember her saying that evening. Her eyes closed. I tried to open them but to no avail. She had fallen back into her deep sleep.

"Momma, listen, I know you will be there with me. You have always been there with me and that is all that matters," I said. It was a long night. There had been many long nights. As I said earlier, I talked to her because I was convinced, she could hear and understand what I was saying.

After I had returned from my brother Paul's home in December and after I went back to complete my finals for that semester of work, I enrolled in the Fresno High School Adult Program. I only needed one class to graduate. Since it was an adult school most of the classes were in the evening. I looked through the schedule of courses and one stood out. It was a public speaking course taught on Tuesday evenings from 5:00 p.m. until 8:00 p.m. I had done some public speaking competitions in high school and thought that this class would help me prepare for college.

Mr. Lindley was the instructor. He taught both day and evening classes at Fresno High School for over 36 years. The classroom was in Brown Hall; named for Governor Pat Brown. There were many types of students enrolled in the course. Most of them were older, but some were in their early twenties. I was the youngest student enrolled in the course.

One of our first assignments was to give a current events speech about something that was happening in the news at either the local, state, or national level. After the assignment, he recognized the two best speakers.

I was one of them while the other outstanding speech was from an eighty-two year old woman who had been attending classes for over fifteen years. She had been taking one class per semester and this was her last high school class before earning her degree.

Mr. Lindley asked the two of us to stay after class. He had to choose the student speaker for graduation and wanted to know if either of us would be interested in being that speaker. The older student said that being the speaker would make her entire academic dream come true. Her dedication and wonderful personality demonstrated to me that dreams can come true. I agreed; she should give the graduation speech.

Graduation night arrived and I went to my graduation alone. At least I thought I was alone. To my knowledge, none of the rest of my family planned to attend. A young couple who had recently joined our church had become my very good friends in a short period of time. They were only about ten years older than I, and it seemed that I could really identify with them. They told me they would try to make it to the graduation ceremony.

We marched down the aisle of the auditorium at Fresno High School. I was shocked when I saw Momma sitting there in the back of the auditorium in a wheelchair. She had come to watch her son graduate.

Part of me wanted to slip out of line and run to her to show her how much it meant to me to have her present at this ceremony. I was surprised that I did not see any of my brothers or sisters there with her. I could not figure out how she had gotten here by herself. The proctors on each side of the stage were directing us into the area where we needed to go. I had never walked so proudly in my life. When they called my name, "Ronald Reel," I walked to the middle of the stage and took my diploma. I looked out into the audience; all the way to the back of the lower level and saw Momma sitting there just as proud as every other mother.

I walked back to my seat with the diploma in my hand. I squeezed it very hard, convincing myself I had completed everything. I took one last glance to the back of the auditorium; but Momma was gone. There was no wheelchair to be seen.

When the ceremony was over, I rushed outside to see if, perhaps, she was still there. I could not find her anywhere. Robert and Bobbi approached me. They had driven into Fresno from Selma. They handed me a present and said there was cake and ice cream waiting for me at their home if I wanted to drop by later. I was very appreciative of their spending the evening trying to make me feel special. It must have been a bit of a sacrifice for them to get a babysitter and take the time to find and purchase a gift. "Thanks, for going to all the extra expense and trouble, but I want to go to the hospital first to check on Momma. If I finish early enough, I will try to come by to thank you for all your support," I said.

I could not find Momma anywhere. My mind must have played some type of trick on me. If someone had hooked me up to a lie detector, I was sure I would pass if I were asked, did I see Momma at my graduation. I didn't see any other family member, but I was sure she had been there watching.

I went to the hospital. Apparently, some commotion was just ending when I arrived. Momma was hooked up to an I.V. I learned that although it was against the doctor's orders, and against everyone's will, Momma had tried to leave the hospital. She had been fighting with the entire staff for the past few hours trying to check herself out.

My sister Nellie informed me that Momma had regained consciousness and had fought with all of them to allow her to leave and go to Fresno High School. Momma had been fighting so long and so hard, she had fallen back into some type of coma. I bent down and kissed her on the cheek. "Thanks Momma. The greatest gift of all was having you there." I took her hand and held it. I asked Nellie for an update on Momma's vital conditions like blood pressure, pulse, heart rate, just to name a few of the items we had all become familiar with as we stayed night after night. The nursing staff had been teaching us what the various numbers meant.

Nellie told me there was a new nurse on the floor and she would not give us the usual information the other staff members provided. It dawned on me that if the nurse covering the station was new, I might be able to find out the information myself. I put on my beauty college smock, which I had left in Momma's room, and said, "Well, it's worth a try." I went out of her room and down the corridors. I looked at the clock above the nurse's station. It was 10:15 p.m. A nurse I had not seen before was sitting at a desk, charting information on one of the other patients.

"Nurse," I said. She looked up, slightly startled that a doctor would be making rounds at this late hour.

"I am Doctor Hardy. Mrs. Reel is one of my patients. I just stopped by her room and found that she has accelerated to a non-coaxial existence with the intravenous setup and her vital signs seem to be parenthetically slumbering and altering. I want to know what is going on," I said.

She looked bewildered. I guess I had said a mouthful of nothings so convincingly, that she handed me Momma's chart and said, "Doctor, most of the physiological changes were exacerbated by the extreme fatigue she suffered from trying to check herself out and leave the hospital to attend some stupid high school graduation ceremony for one of her sons." I was deep in concentration trying to understand all of the comments on the chart, but I heard her comment about the graduation ceremony. "Doctor, don't you think if that son loved her, he would have insisted his mother stay here in bed where she belongs?" she asked.

"Perhaps the son did not know his mother would try to attend the ceremony," I replied.

"She kept saying she could see him graduating from where she was sitting. I guess she eventually thought she was at the ceremony."

"This graduation may have been the driving force keeping her alive for these past painful months. Who are we to judge? We can't change what took place. Let us embrace why it took place. Maybe for a short time she ignored the pain by making herself believe she was attending the graduation. Our minds are very powerful. She willed herself to see her son graduate. She knew it was today and as far as I am concerned, she was in attendance," I said.

"Yes, Doctor," she said. I turned and walked back to Momma's room. I closed the door. Nellie and I read through the charts making sense of as much as we were able to decipher from the notes and abbreviations. We arrived at the following conclusion. Momma had just performed a feat that perplexed and intrigued the local medical community. She had come back to reality for about two hours. She was coherent and was serious about leaving the hospital to complete a promise she had made. The combination of physical and mental strain had caused her momentary excitement and eventually exhaustion.

By the time I returned the chart to the nurse's station, one of the regular nurses was working. I should have returned while the new nurse was still there. I was caught.

"Sometime during the evening, someone must have left this chart in Momma's room," I said.

"Yes!" she said. "A Doctor Hardy, I believe."

"Well, you know me. I can't tell one doctor from the other. They all look alike with those white coats," I said. She winked and smiled at me.

"Let me put that back where it belongs in case any of the other doctors need to see information concerning your mother, Dr. Hardy," she said.

I went back to Momma's room. About 2:00 a.m. Momma began to shiver and cry out. I can still hear her today.

"Ronald, will you hold my hand?" she asked.

"Of course. I have hold of your hand right now. I am here Momma," I said.

"Hold my hand because I am scared," she said softly.

"There is nothing to be scared of Momma. Remember when I was young and you held my hand? There wasn't anything to be scared of because you were there. I am here now."

"Please do me a favor," she said whispering almost inaudibly.

"Sure, you name it and I will do it," I agreed.

"Remember when you were scared of the dark? You were not afraid when I was there with you. Promise me you or one of the other kids will be here holding my hand at night. Will you promise me?" she asked. How could I say no? Once she had been there for me. I made sure that on the fourth night when I returned home to sleep in my own bed, someone else was there to hold her hand.

She slipped back into a coma. It was just like a trance. She didn't talk. She couldn't see. We could see her. We could hear her. We saw the tears streaming from her eyes because of the pain that could not be lessened with the maximum of drugs she was allowed. We heard her cough. We heard her scream out in pain from time to time. We heard her whimper. We felt her body getting colder as her lungs filled with fluid. We hoped she would get better. We did not want her to die; but we did not want her to continue to suffer.

Sunday morning dawned bright and sunny, my sister, Nellie, arrived at the hospital to sit with Momma. She was going to stay the day shift. As I drove to church, my mind began playing tricks on me. I could not concentrate on any one thing. My constantly absent Father, and my dying Mother caused me to return to a time in my life when I was afraid of everything. It was the first time I had rheumatic fever and I thought I was going to die.

My older brothers teased me about being the adopted member of the family. I wanted to be a full-fledged member, not just someone who had been adopted. They had told me I had been left on the doorstep the night my twin was born. I knew that statement was not true. Aunt Dovie and Momma had never varied from their story of our births. My siblings claimed that Momma had told the older kids that adopting me was not difficult because one more mouth to feed would not make a difference.

Suddenly my mind went back to the first grade when our teacher asked us to find out our nationality. I thought it might be a problem since there was a possibility I had been left on the doorstep. I wanted to find out as much as possible about my nationality. I remember asking Momma what I thought was a very important question: "Momma, what am I?"

"Well, you're a boy," Momma replied.

"No, I am not that crazy. I mean, what do we have in us?" I quizzed.

"Supper is almost ready. Will this take long?" she asked impatiently.

"No, that is all I need to know," I said. Momma was busy taking out the biscuits and burning her finger on the side of the pan.

"We are a little of everything like most people. Some say we are American Indian because of my side of the family. Some say we are Irish because of your Dad's side. But I like to say we are Airedale," she said. I had always thought we were Cherokee like Momma's family. My teacher had not named Airedale as a possible nationality.

"That is neat!" I said. This new nationality was going to make me special tomorrow. The next day I waited with bated breath for the teacher to begin Family Answer Time. One student said she was Scandinavian. Another student said his family was Australian. One last student said he was All-American. Finally, she called on me.

"Ronald, what nationality are you?" she inquired.

"We are Airedale," I said. I was expecting complete surprise and joy. Instead of the delightful smile Mrs. Jenner usually displayed, her brow was raised up and her voice was louder than usual.

"What did you say?" she pressed.

"Airedale!" I reiterated.

"I don't think you are taking this assignment seriously," she said. She stood and moved away from her desk toward me.

"Would you like to apologize to the class?" she insisted.

"I asked Momma last night like you said to do. That is what I was told," I said.

"You asked your Mother your nationality and this is the reply you were given?"

"Yes Ma'am. Is something wrong?" I asked.

"Not if your parents are dogs," stated the teacher. I did not know how to react. I thought I had followed the instructions given to me.

"Mrs. Jenner, are you calling my family names?" I asked.

"No! You are doing that yourself," she retorted.

"I don't understand."

"An Airedale is a dog," she said. I could hear snickering coming from my classmates.

"I am very sorry Mrs. Jenner. My mother must have misunderstood my question. I'll know for sure tomorrow," I said. I couldn't believe that I had made such a fool of myself. I couldn't believe that Momma had told me something so wrong. Maybe I had been adopted and it was too painful for my family to admit.

During that evening, I tried to get the nerve to ask why I had been given such wrong information. At one point I asked Donald to ask what type of Indian Reservation Momma lived on before she and Father married and moved to California. I thought that would be the appropriate time to clear up the nationality question. When I told them about the Airedale answer, Momma began to laugh and then when she saw my face, she began apologizing for her statement the previous night. She had been in a hurry to get dinner on the table and she thought I was just passing time. I think she said something about me pestering her while she was cooking.

"Son, I thought you knew that an Airedale was a dog. I am sorry. Do you want me to talk to your teacher tomorrow and tell her I did say that to you! I can write a note if you like." For the rest of my life when people asked me about my nationality, I always silently responded to myself, "I am Airedale."

Just then a car turned in front of me and caused me to return to the real world. I wasn't five or six or nine or ten. I was eighteen. I had just graduated from high school and was almost through with my technical training in cosmetology. I had accomplished much. I made it to church just in time to hear the choir sing and to hear a sermon about forgiveness and courage. It was time to head back to the hospital.

I left church and drove my 1958 Chevrolet back to the hospital to check on Momma. This was the same car my brother-in law Raymond had helped me purchase last summer. He had help me get it because it was cheap, was running, easy to repair, and from the car lot where he worked as a mechanic. He was a master mechanic at Great Auto Deals in Fresno. I bought the car with money I earned working weekends and evenings when possible at Beefy Burgers, a fast-food restaurant that sold hamburgers and hot dogs. He and his oldest son, my nephew Percy, only four years younger than I, completely fine-tuned the engine for me. They made sure it was in good running condition so I would have transportation while attending college. The car cost only one hundred dollars and they let me make payments for four months to pay it off. At the hospital I expected to meet up with some of my older siblings. Two of my married sisters and two married brothers were bringing their families into town because we felt the end for Momma was close.

I had not expected Father to be there, but there he was standing in the lobby. It turned out he had come to see me. The ranch owner he worked for had told him he could no longer drive the company pickup. The owner felt Father was a capable mechanic, but he was a poor driving risk off the land, which he knew so well. His boss had told him he could drive the truck during working hours, but at the end of the day, he had to give the truck back. He could only drive on their property.

I heard my Father's voice. "Ronald!" he called. I turned around and he came up beside me.

"Why are you here? What do you want?" I asked. He looked at me coldly with his dark eyes. His stance was almost stiff, as though he were standing at attention.

"I want the keys to your car," he said.

"Why do you need my keys?"

"Because I want to go home," he said in a concise and urgent manner.

"Nellie is here at the hospital. I can get her to take you home. A couple of the boys are here; or will be here soon. I can get one of them to take you home. I need my car because when I leave the hospital tonight, I will go home and sleep, drive back to beauty school in the morning, and be back here at the hospital tomorrow night after finishing with everything," I explained.

He looked straight forward into my eyes. "I...want...your...car!" he yelled.

"Father, I can get one of the other kids to take you home," I said. Suddenly he slapped me across the face as hard as he could hit. I landed in the middle of the floor in the lobby waiting room. All eyes of those people waiting to see friends, relatives, or loved ones focused on us; those people waiting to see a doctor, and those people who had driven someone else to the hospital fixed their eyes on the sideshow taking place in the lobby. I looked up at Father.

"I said, I want your car!" he yelled at me again.

"It is my car," I repeated.

"Give me the keys to the car you been tellin people is yours. I bought that car!" he screamed at the top of his voice.

"You didn't buy the car. I paid for it with my own money I earned working extra jobs," I said.

"I bought that car," said Father.

"You know I paid for that car last summer. I just bought brand new tires for it, so I won't worry about driving back and forth from college to visit. That is the car I am taking to college with me," I said. By this time, I had gotten off the floor and was standing looking directly into his eyes. Slap! Once again, the man who fathered me chose to display his discontent with his son in a public setting, exhibiting a brutal communication strategy.

"I said I want that car now! Give me the keys to the car!" Father said. He placed his hands directly around my neck. The pressure from his rough fingers was penetrating the flesh. As I spoke, I could feel the pressure cutting off my breathing ability.

"It is my car," I reiterated.

"I want you to give me that car," he said emphasizing each word.

"It is my car. I paid for it," I said for the third or fourth time. I felt like standing up to Father, but I did not think that the hospital was the right place to do it. Besides, his large hands continued to strangle me. I had never seen him so aggressive.

"I want the keys!" he said again. Fumbling in my pockets, I found the keys. I handed them to him.

"Here, here are the keys," I said. Father let go of me. Again, I fell to the floor. He began to walk toward the exit doors leading to the parking lot. He turned back towards me one last time.

"I don't want you to be in my house when I get home tonight! Is that understood? I want you gone. I don't care where you go. I just don't want you in my home," he said.

"Don't worry. You have my car. I hope it makes you happy. I won't be in your house when you get, no, if you make it home tonight. You know what? I have always tried not to talk back, but you're going to hear what I have to say right now," I screamed. I ran in front of him. I was at the exit door which he had to go through in order to get to his new car. The door slid open.

"Now if you don't want to hear this, then just slap me again here in front of all these people. Just one warning; you better be ready for a fight this time. You are never going to run over me again! This little sassy son of yours will try his best to beat the living daylights out of you even if you are my father," I said shaking uncontrollably. Father stood half-stunned, half-amazed, and totally caught off guard.

"I don't know who you are anymore. You strut in here and scream and we all try to jump at your every command. Well, I quit. I'm not going to jump for you anymore. I hope this little escapade makes you feel really good, and I hope it soothes your threatened manhood because your wife is upstairs in the hospital, and she is dying. I am not going to continue telling her lies about how you have sneaked up and she was asleep and had been kissed by you, and how much you miss her because you love her so much. You want to know why? Because you can't love anybody but yourself. I am going to tell her the truth from this moment on," I said. Father just stood saying nothing. All of the people looking at us just stood there spellbound. Not one person had gone to call the police or security.

"I am going to tell her that instead of you being with her, you are out with other women. All your children are turning on you. You have three kids right now that need a father because they are afraid their mother is dying. None of them, us, have a father to help them through this very difficult time. We didn't ask to be brought into this world, and I know you didn't want us, but we are here now. Be a man. Be the father I know you can be. I can take care of myself. I am going to make it somehow. You have two little girls who need somebody today, tonight, every night. It is not their fault and they should not be punished. I have said all I am going to say. This conversation is over. Our relationship is over," I said. One by one the onlookers began to focus back on why they had originally come to the hospital.

"The show is over." I said to the people still watching. "Please forgive us for publicly demonstrating this unacceptable behavior. I am truly sorry anyone had to see this," I said in almost a whispered voice.

As I walked out of St. Luke's Hospital after fighting with Father, I paid no attention to the cars on either side of the streets and highway as I walked to Pastor DeWolfe's house. I could not focus nor see anything or think clearly. All I could hear were his words, "Give me the keys to your car. Get out of my house. When I get home, I don't want to find you there. I want you out."

CHAPTER ELEVEN

I didn't want to fight Father any longer at the hospital, so I began walking down the street I had driven so many times in recent months. I walked, and walked, and walked. I tried to think of a happy time when Father had seemed gentle, kind, and caring. I searched for a time when we had been a family. Then it came to me. It was Christmas a few years earlier.

The Christmas tree sat so proudly in the corner of our living room. Its branches were full, and its radiant smell aroused everyone's anticipation of Christmas cheer. Each of us at home had contributed our own special ornament for the tree. Together we had made a chain for the tree from different scraps of paper from around the house. We had cut the paper into even strips, pasted them with flour glue, and had written special messages in crayon on the outside concerning giving, caring, and loving one another. Underneath the tree was wrapped boxes. Most of the them were empty. We had wrapped empty boxes so the older married children would not realize our financial need was as desperate as it actually was that year.

Momma had called us all together the week before and said, "Why don't we do something special this year? Your father and I haven't been able to work much, so money is pretty tight. I don't know if we'll be able to get ya kids much, but I do promise a real nice meal. Why don't each of ya find a picture of what ya would get each of us if ya could afford it. Then, put that picture in a box, wrap it up, and put it under the tree. Right before we open the presents, you can ask the giver why that particular gift was chosen for you. Alright?"

I knew the girls wanted dresses. I looked through the catalogs and magazines at various stores and at doctors' offices trying to find the special "gift." My twin wanted a bicycle. Father always got a shirt from each of the older six brothers and sisters. So, I made sure his present was something different. I got him a picture of a radio. I wanted him to have some music to listen to when he worked out in the fields. He was usually working by 5:30 a.m. and did not return home until about 7:00 p.m. It was hard to decide on Momma's gift. She had so little, yet she gave so much. Finally, I decided to get her one of those new make-up kits that had lipstick and other cosmetics in it. She always said that she wished she had stuff to make her look prettier when, occasionally, she and my father went someplace special on a Saturday night, "out-on-the-town" they called it.

The "gifts" were cute and amusing. We laughed and laughed. It was very entertaining to see what each one of us thought the other siblings should have if money was not an object. Finally, the time came for the grand finale! The real gifts! My twin and two younger sisters had agreed upon a one-dollar limit on the gifts we were giving to each other. The four of us had decided to spend two dollars on each of our parents.

I had saved a pair of gloves given to me the year before by my parents. For the past year I kept my hands inside my pockets instead of wearing them. I did this to provide my twin with his present which, therefore, did not cost me any money. This also allowed me to spend more money on Momma's gift. Both of the girls received underwear and a dress. Their dresses were not as pretty as the picture "gifts," but I thought the girls were as pretty in their dresses as the models displaying the catalog dresses.

The four of us had put our money together so that we could get our parents something special. We wanted Father to open his present first.

"Father, this is your gift from all of us," said Frances, the youngest. She was eight.

"You mean I only get one gift?" Father asked jokingly.

"Yeah, but it's special! We were able to spend more because we pooled our money together Father," said Karen. She was eleven. Father unwrapped his gift. He held up a new pair of Levi's.

"Well, will ya look there. I'll be struttin up a storm in those pants," he said.

Karen couldn't wait. "Momma, quick, close your eyes and hold out your hand."

As Momma started to obey Karen, my twin Donald, interrupted, "You guys slow down. You're getting ahead. We're supposed to give them the Christmas card we made first. Ok?"

I had been asked to read the card we had made. We had taken two brown grocery bags and cut them, so we had two equal-sized papers shaped like an ornament. Scraps found in Momma's quilting box had been glued to the sides to add color. We had written a verse on the inside, expressing our love to them. I opened the card and began to read:

HAPPY CHRISTMAS, MOM AND DAD

WE HOPE THIS CARD MAKES YOU GLAD

YOU GIVE US SO MUCH

THERE IS NO REASON TO BE SAD

YOU WORK SO HARD TO TRY AND PLEASE US

WE WISH YOU WOULDN'T MAKE SUCH A FUSS

OUR GIFTS TO YOU AREN'T MUCH

BUT AT LEAST IT IS SOMETHING TO TOUCH

WE LOVE YOU VERY MUCH

Momma was really impressed with the card. "You children are the best children in the whole town," she said.

Frances could not hold our gift for Momma secret any longer, and she insisted, "Momma, you have to open your gift right now." Karen handed Momma a large package. We had asked Nellie, our oldest sister, what she thought Momma would like if we could give her an actual gift. Nellie told us she would take the money we had collected and purchase the gift for us. When she brought it back to us, the gift was already wrapped. Nellie told us that this way it would be our secret too and we would be as surprised as Momma when she opened it. Because she was the oldest, because she was a mother, and because she had children of her own, we knew she would make a good choice. Momma looked at the wrapping. The gift had been professionally wrapped. It was not a brown bag with crayon colors; instead, it was bright shiny gold and red.

"This box is so pretty; I don't know if I can open it. The box itself is enough for me," she exclaimed. We all said at the same time, "No, open it." Momma gently set the gift on the kitchen table and got a knife from the cupboard so she could cut the paper to preserve it so it could be used again. After almost surgically removing the cover, Momma found another box inside the pretty outside box. There was a handwritten note on it. She read it silently at first, and then smiled and read aloud, "Open this box knowing how much your children, who gave all they had to make your holiday special, love you. This gift will accent your true beauty." Momma looked at each of us as she opened the inside box. It was a dress that had a matching jacket. It was beautiful. None of us had ever seen a dress this formal or this beautiful. Collectively, we sighed in disbelief at what the money we had given Nellie could buy. We never found out how much additional money she had contributed, but Nellie helped make this a very special day for our special Momma.

Not only had we shared presents, we also shared a love experienced in the deepest family way. Momma was right when she said, "Poverty cannot take away respect and love, because respect for self and others cannot be bought with money." With outstretched hands, Momma called us to her side. She placed us in a circle and asked us to hold hands. "Today is Christmas, she exclaimed. "I know that we're not real religious, but we are a real family. I want us to each bow our heads and Ronald you lead us in a Christmas Prayer. Sometimes I think we have failed you kids because we can't give ya what some of the other parents give their children. But, today, I feel we have more than any other family in this town. We have each other. You children are the most important things in our lives. Whether we can give ya gifts, or buy ya clothes, or send ya on trips, we'll always give ya love and stand behind whatever you decide to do." I know each of ya are gonna make it in this world. Ronald, ya ready to pray?" she asked.

"Sure," I said.

"Jesus, we are so lucky today. We want to thank you for letting us live together. We want you to know that we are real proud to be a family. Thanks for giving us a Father, who works hard and does his very best to give us nice things. Thanks for a Mother, who sits up at night with us when we are sick and takes care of us each day. Thanks for Karen, Frances, and Donald. Thanks for our family. We know that Christmas is a time when people share presents, but the real reason is because of You. Thanks for being born and living your life so that through your dying on the cross we have a way to being saved," I prayed .

For a brief moment, we sat squeezing hands and feeling the electric energy flowing bountifully from each one independently to all collectively. We were a unit. Even Father was moved. This was the first time he pulled us all together and embraced us with his solid grasp. The squeeze was hard and firm. His voice was shaky and weak:

"I don't usually say much; your Ma does most of the talkin to ya kids. But, I just thought ya oughta know, I...I... lo..."

I waited hopefully for him to say the word.

"Well, I...love...ya...all," he blurted out.

Contained within that moment was the element that makes a family worthwhile. We were sheltered in a warm bath of love; for on this very special day was brought to us a very special gift that none had expected. Father had said that he loved us.

My knocking at Pastor DeWolfe's front door brought me back to reality. I had been walking several hours, from the hospital in Fresno to Clovis. I allowed my eyes to shed tears because it hurt to know that the Reel family was no longer. Father could not handle the cancer Momma was experiencing, nor was he prepared for her imminent death.

I told Pastor DeWolfe everything that had happened in the last twenty-four hours. He was especially shocked when I told him about Father taking my car and that I had walked all the way to his house from Fresno. Pastor said he had a Honda motorcycle that I could use as long as I needed to, until I left for college. He made me promise to use the helmet that he gave me to wear whenever I would ride it. I did not know how to express my gratitude or astonishment at his generosity.

He told me, "You can't be expected to finish all the loose items this summer without having transportation. I know you will take care of the bike and am not worried. I will keep up the insurance and you need to know it gets great gas mileage." He hugged me and told me how proud of me he was for staying the course and standing up for the values that matter. He offered me one last thought, "Your father is a better man than he looks right now. His entire world has fallen apart. Remember the good things that you had with him, your mom, and your brothers and sisters. He just does not know how to respond to any of the situation at hand." I wanted to try to forgive Father for what he had done to me. I would try to be the bigger of the two. At that time, however, I did not know what Father was about to do that would convince me he was very selfish and did not care about his family.

The next day as I arrived at the hospital riding my new Honda, I saw my three older brothers and Father standing in front of the hospital entrance. I parked the motorcycle and began walking in their direction. They resembled characters from a Western movie, standing and protecting those inside from any intruders. Brandon, the eldest, was, probably, six feet three and weighed two hundred and sixty pounds. He worked in construction and he was solid muscle. Harry was closest in age to me. He stood six feet one and weighed more than two hundred pounds. He was known as the rowdy one. He loved to fight. Paul, the middle brother, was a Golden Gloves boxing champion. Even though he was only five feet ten inches tall, he was much huskier than I. Father seemed smothered between my brothers. Although he was in his late fifties, the years he had spent down in the coal mines had toned his body so much that any man his age would be proud of it. They were standing side by side blocking the entry, keeping me from Momma.

Harry spoke first, "We hear there was some trouble yesterday." I didn't know what to say because I didn't know what Father had told them. Not one time since Momma had been in the hospital had all of them been in attendance at the same time. I tried to establish momentary eye contact with each of them. I did my best to look into their eyes searching for the truth that might be there. During this brief encounter, I tried to imagine what Father had told them.

"I guess you're right," I said. Harry began moving toward me. Of all the brothers, he was the one I felt was most likely to listen to logic, if I could get my story out before him. I had never had any reason to lie or to find myself in any type of altercation with any of them. When they needed a babysitter, I always volunteered. If they had any type of paperwork that needed to be examined by any agency like child services, welfare, or the courts, I always read, explained, and helped them with a written response.

"We don't think it was very wise to tell Dad off in front of all them people in the waiting room," he said

"You are probably right. I guess I shouldn't have said what I..." Paul broke through before I could continue my sentence.

"We don't think you should have said what you said. Period!" he added. At this moment, Father moved to the back of the pack. My brothers were moving towards me in what I thought resembled a mob.

Well, I think I said what was needed," I protested. Each set of eyes suddenly glared at me. I felt like I was soon to be crushed physically again. This time it was going to happen outside of the hospital. Father had convinced my brothers I had not only disrespected him, but had screamed uncontrollably, and had attacked him physically. I was the debater, the dramatist, the orator. I solved problems through logic, strategy, and other verbal means. I had never gotten into any type of physical confrontation in my life. Father now began moving toward the front of the lynch mob.

"Ronald, you have always been different. The boys and me were always afraid to treat you like we did one another. I just never could talk to ya. I never could tell you the way it is cause you never can see things the way they really are, boy. You always try to imagine things big and fancy the way you like them to be. You never could make a decision by yourself. You always had to talk it over with ya Ma," he said. Harry interrupted Father: "You pulled a big blooper yesterday! You had no right calling Dad names in front of all them people. Telling him he had no education, and that he couldn't provide good enough for you all cause he was ignorant and poor. How do you like it when you're called names?" he added. I wondered what, if anything, I could say to help them know what had really happened last night. I decided I had taken all I could.

"Now, you all just back off for a minute. Wait just one minute." I was going to say what I had to say. "None of the rest of you were involved. I think what was said should be taken care of between Father and me. However, since you were brought into this matter, I think it is time you heard the truth about what happened.

Father, I told you yesterday I wasn't going to lie for you anymore. Why don't you tell my brothers the truth about who did what to whom and who said what to whom?" I said. By this time, I was raising my voice. Our family was used to loud arguments, which many times wound up in physical confrontation. Father tried to sluff off my attack concerning his truthfulness.

"Boy, I think we can settle this without a whole lotta trouble, don't you? Look boys, he just got mad. He didn't mean any of those things he said. He was just blowin off some steam."

"Father, I meant every single word I said. You were the one mad and screaming. You are the one who did the hitting. Why don't you scream some of those same things you said to me right now? Father aren't you man enough?" I said. My brothers grabbed me. One had me from behind. One stood between Father and myself while the other brother grabbed my arms. I managed to push them away.

"Get your hands off me, NOW! I don't have anything against any of you. Father is the one who is trying to cause trouble between us. He slapped me and he made me give him the keys to my car. He can have it. He wants his freedom from being a responsible parent. He can have it, but he is not going to make me out a liar. Not now, and not ever again," I avowed.

"None of you have been at this hospital night after night. Father, you know that you have not been here either. None of you know how many nights Father did not show up because he was out at some bar with only, he knows whom. I lied to Momma, telling her he had visited and had left to rest so he could go on providing for us. Father, why don't you tell your sons here where you have been every night?" I asked.

My brothers seemed puzzled. They had never seen me so assertive and so in control of a situation. I figured I should continue while I had their attention. I felt this might be the only opportunity I would have to express myself to all of them at the same time.

"I grant you are all bigger and stronger than I. But, none of you are more of a man than I am. Now, I might not measure up to you by your standards. I am not very physical. I can be emotional. There is not one of you who will prevent me from walking through those doors and going up to be with our Mother.

Now you better get out of my way, and you better not touch me as I walk through that entrance because I have been here all the time and you haven't. By my books, that gives me the right to see her. I may not be able to live at home because Father doesn't want me there, but I am free to go see Momma and none of you have any right to prevent me from entering this hospital," I concluded.

As my feet moved forward, my thoughts were ranging from what to do when they grabbed for me to how fast I should run for the door. I suddenly remembered how I had seen them all fight with other people, their spouses, even with their friends from time to time. I was no match for any of my brothers individually, and certainly I was not a match for them collectively.

For an instant, I wondered how I would get up off the ground if I had the ability to do so, after they stopped hitting me. To my great surprise and relief, they moved to the side and I entered the hospital without further problems.

Later that night as I sat holding Momma's hand, I fell asleep. Suddenly, I was awakened by her violently moving arm. I thought that perhaps she was having some type of a nightmare.

"Momma, it is O.K., I am here. I am holding your hand. There is nothing to worry about." I said. Suddenly she sat up in the hospital bed. Her eyes opened. She started to gasp for air like she had been under water and needed to take a breath of air.

"Ronald, Ronald?" she asked for me by name.

"Momma, I am here. I'm here," I told her.

"Go call all of my children and tell them if they want to see me alive, they better come now," she said. The doctors had told us she would never regain consciousness. Obviously, they were wrong. But I was not sure what was taking place in Room 624 of St. Luke's Hospital. My first instinct was to ignore the validity of her knowledge of being so near to death. I wanted to make sure I had not fallen asleep and was hallucinating or dreaming. I began asking myself to focus and see if what was happening was real or not.

"Momma don't be silly. You aren't going to die. All of your children are nearby. We're waiting for you to get well," I said. I leaned over the bed to try and get her to recline back to a more relaxed position. As I pushed her gently back, she spoke again.

"Please do this one last favor, son, please!" she whispered. She closed her eyes and fell back into unconsciousness. I drew her hand toward me. I kissed it lightly. Then I placed her hand back beside her body. For a moment my thoughts were full of the day's events. How would this call be received by those still upset with me? What if she wasn't dying? What if I had just imagined all this? What if I were the one who had lost touch with reality? Maybe I could trade places with her. Perhaps I should be admitted to the hospital as a mental patient because I finally cracked under the pressure of all I was doing. My head was already bowed as I began to pray.

"Lord God, you are a loving and caring Creator. Today has been the most difficult day of my life. Once You granted me the opportunity to share with Momma your commandments and she reaffirmed you as her Savior. Yet, my, our family has disappeared, dissolved, disintegrated. Is there any possible way I can take on her illness? She is needed far more by others that I am. Most of my family wouldn't care much if were alive or dead. I think my two younger sisters really need a mother more than they need a brother. If you take me, they will still have four brothers. That's more than most people have. The girls will need a new mother. They deserve to be loved and made to feel special. I cannot do that for them," I said.

Suddenly I heard a voice that was as loud as Momma's when she had spoken to me. "Have I not led you through many trials and tribulations thus far in your short life? You have a special duty and reason for living the life I have given you. All things work together. Be patient and don't question my ability for providing. You will always be taken care of as long as you trust me. Let go of the other children. They are not your responsibility. Their lives will be better off because of this situation. Each child will discover love and caring. You are to be only their brother. Now, do as your Mother has requested. I will never forsake you," the voice promised.

Some will never be convinced that God spoke to me and it is not my desire to convince anyone of what happened on that night so long ago. For some it will be a delusion. Others will make it even more dramatic than it was. All I can say is that I lived it. It was my reality at that time.

I looked down at Momma lying there in bed. Her head was in the middle of the pillow. Her eyes were closed, and now there were no tears of pain. She looked rested, peaceful, and serene. I walked out of her room, down to the end of the corridor, and began stuffing coins into the pay telephone. I called each one of her children and told them what Momma had requested for me to tell them. There were various responses.

"Hi, sorry to call so late. Momma came out of the coma and asked me to call each of you. She said if you want to see her alive, come to the hospital soon," I said to each one.

"Didn't the doctors say she could live a couple more weeks?" asked Harry.

"I am not going to argue what the doctors told us. All I am doing is what Momma asked me to do. You don't have to come if you don't want to. She asked me to call all of her children; and that is what I am doing. Do what you want. Goodbye," I said. I stayed at that telephone booth until I had called everyone. A couple of them came to the hospital.

At seven the next morning, I had to leave to go to beauty school. It was customary that upon completion of my theory class, I would call the hospital and check on Momma's condition. Nine o'clock, just like clockwork, I would call. Today, however, theory class ran late, and I had several appointments waiting for me. I set their hair very quickly, using my famous (at least I called it that) five rollers set, put them under the dryer, and set the timers a little longer than usual. Once this had been done, I called the hospital. I had learned many months ago how to bypass the operator. I knew the direct line to the nurses' station on the sixth floor. The nurse's name was Vera.

"Good morning Vera. I'm just calling to check up on Momma. Has her condition changed this morning?" I asked. The traditional response was that she was still in critical condition, but her present condition was stable. Today there was absolute silence.

"Vera, I am checking up on Mrs. Reel." It seemed like an eternity while I waited for an answer. There was no sound, no response. There was dead silence. "Oh, honey, your mother expired this morning at seven fifteen," she said. I didn't think I heard her correctly. Momma had died and not one person called me.

"Can you tell me if the family has been notified?" I questioned.

"Yes, the immediate family number was called. They said they could get hold of the rest of you. They have probably been trying to call you," she said very compassionately. I didn't know what to do. Had I merely been overlooked?

It had been over two hours since Momma had died. Suddenly, my private thoughts were no longer hidden from view. My feelings were on public display. Mrs. Nordon was standing beside me as I held the phone in my hand. I spoke softly into it, "Thank you very much. Thanks for putting up with my calls every day. I'll miss talking with you," I said to Vera. The feeling of total abandonment combined with complete isolation is hard to describe. It was as though my heart stopped beating. I was angry because no one had called. I was hurt because Momma was gone. I felt alone because I had not been there to hold her hand. I looked directly into Mrs. Nordon's eyes.

"Ma'am, I'd like to be excused to go home today, please," I requested. She could tell something was very wrong.

"What's the matter?" she asked. I had always thought of Mrs. Nordon as a mother figure. She had a soft heart; but she could be harsh when needed, especially if she thought someone was not living up to her standard of professionalism.

"My Mother is dead. She died this morning, and they didn't even call and let me know. She is finally gone. At least she's not suffering any more. Mrs. Nordon, I know she is happier and better off than she was; but it hurts," I said. Mrs. Nordon pulled me close and hugged me as though I were her child. By this time, a few of the other students had noticed me and were coming to give me strength and courage during this low point of my life. I didn't have to say anything to them. I knew their love was present and that was sufficient for me.

"You go ahead and take the day off, Ronald, and you come back when you're good and ready. If I can help you or you need anything at all, just call me," she said.

"Thank your Mrs. Nordon. I will be back soon," I responded.

I went outside, put my helmet on, and mounted the Honda motorcycle. The same questions kept repeating in my mind. Why couldn't it have been me? Why wasn't I the one to die? Perhaps some car would hit me as I drove away from the beauty college and I could be exchanged for her.

I knew I would have to be strong so the others could get through what was about to happen. I directed the motorcycle toward Father's house. It was no longer our home, but just a house.

When I arrived there, many of my brothers and sisters were already present. The others were on their way. It was a difficult moment. I suddenly felt estranged. I saw all of the others feeling sad, hurt, crying; but I did not dare to show any emotion.

Because I was the only regular churchgoer in the family and they wanted Momma to have a religious funeral service, the rest of the family wanted me to take care of getting pallbearers, a singer, and a preacher. They also left it up to me to take care of all the logistics of the funeral itself. Father and Brandon went to the cemetery to secure a plot and make the financial arrangements to pay for the burial. After they returned from the cemetery, I learned they did not have enough money to pay for a tombstone or permanent marker for Momma's grave. They all had agreed to contribute some funds within six months to purchase a headstone. I was afraid it might take at least a year before there would be enough money contributed to purchase a permanent grave marker.

One last request was made. My sisters wanted me to do Momma's hair. I agreed, but I needed to know when she was arriving at the mortuary. I asked to use the phone. I called and was informed she would be there about one o'clock. The manager of the funeral home confirmed 2:00 p.m. as the best time to do her hair.

Not one of my siblings mentioned not calling me earlier in the day to give me the news about Momma. It was a chaotic time for all of us. I don't know how many of them even knew the actual name of my cosmetology college; none of them had ever come by to see me in action or to have their hair done. Maybe they wanted to call me; but did not have a phone number. Each one could have thought one of the others had called. Perhaps they felt there was no rush to call me since there was nothing I could do anyway.

I left what was once our home and rode to the mortuary on my borrowed Honda motorcycle. I had met the owners of the funeral home at various church functions. They were good Christian people. They worked with the poor people in Clovis so that they, too, could bury their loved ones with dignity.

I had been in this building before for other funerals. Somehow, the funeral home looked different on this personal visit. The manager met me as I walked into the main lobby. I thought I was well composed. I had been talking to myself about how this would be the last gift I could give Momma. I had convinced myself that I was ready.

"Hi, I'm Ron Reel. My mother is here," I said. The funeral home manager greeted me with a smile and a professional handshake, firm, but not too firm.

"Let me express our sincere condolences and understanding for you and your family during this difficult time," she said.

"The family wants me to, uh, do her hair and make-up like she would want," I said. This sentence was really not needed. After all, I had made this appointment with her.

"Of course. Mrs. Reel is in the embalming room. Would you like to follow me please?" The manager turned and began to walk down the corridor. As we walked from the lobby into the private section not open to the public, there was an eerie feeling and a sterile smell in the building I had never noticed on previous visits.

"Sure. May I ask a special favor? I have never worked on a dead person before, so, well, because it's my mother, I might need a little assistance. If you can stay in the room with me, I would appreciate it," I told her. We walked further down the corridor and through a door marked "1."

As the door opened and the lights were turned on by a switch near the door, the distinction between the carpeting we had been on and the shiny floor tile we were on now was quite evident. I felt unable to raise my eyes from the floor. My knees suddenly felt weak. I thought I would pass out. I wanted to turn and run, but something deep inside of me said to stay put. The manager looked at me and offered some coping advice for this novice funeral cosmetologist.

"You might want to take a couple of deep breaths and hold on to the side of this receptacle. Sometimes the initial exposure to a dead body is a little difficult.

Remember that the body is dead. Your mother isn't there any longer. This is only the vessel where she lived. Her spirit has left and gone to heaven. You tell me when you're ready. I'll stand here beside you," she said as she completed her instructions.

I prayed silently, "God, please give me extra strength and courage as I attempt this." As I opened my eyes, I began to recognize and single out objects in the room. There were two special embalming tables. These tubs were upright and on hydraulics. The surface looked like porcelain. They were white and occupied. Sheets were covering the bodies.

"Mrs. Reel is on the left," the manager said as I was motioned to move closer.

"Thank you," I replied. The sheet covered her body. The manager pulled the sheet down to reveal Momma's face and shoulder area. As I looked toward her, I was suddenly afraid to touch the body. I tried to tell my legs to move closer, but they would not move. I reached down and placed my hands around one of my legs. I then moved that leg closer to where I wanted to be.

I was now only two feet away from the body on the table. It certainly looked like Momma. The manager had told me it was my mother. Yet, she looked so very strange. Momma's hair had been combed straight back while wet and allowed to dry very close to her scalp. She looked like a mannequin from where I was standing. Suddenly I felt like I was back at the cosmetology college on my first day when I could not get any of the mannequins to cooperate. I knew when I touched her, however, she would not be wooden or rubber. Great fear overcame me. I was afraid to touch her. My eyes must have revealed my shock and concern.

"When we get them in, we place them here until we can fully groom and select what they will wear and then decide on the coffin," said the manager. I was staring at what resembled a water hose or spray hose in a kitchen sink. It all seemed so impersonal.

"See, we spray them down, soap them up, and disinfect them before the embalming. We set their hands in position before rigor mortis prevents such an action, and then we place dentures if they are required to fill the mouth and jawbone lines, wire their mouths shut so they don't open. If they did, then we would have to break the jaw to reset it closed. Sometimes they move during the first few hours we have them. The areas around the eyes, nose, and mouth have a protective cream over them to keep the body as moist as possible. The hair color you ordered, rollers, combs, all those materials are right here. Remember when you set her hair, place cotton or something like that where the band in the plastic dryer cover touches the face. That elastic will leave a mark we can't get out of the skin if you don't cover it."

Perhaps she had forgotten how I was related to this person. I wasn't a trained funeral hair cosmetologist. This was Momma. I felt so helpless. Momma had always cared for others. Now it was impossible for her to care for anyone ever again. The phone at the funeral home began ringing. The manger left the room to answer it. I wanted to leave also. How could I survive in this room with my dead mother unable to respond to me? I reached down to touch her. Somehow, I felt I had to talk to her as I worked. I started talking aloud. My voice echoed throughout the embalming room.

"Momma, I don't know if you're in a place where you can hear me. I hope so, because I want to share some very personal things with you. The reason why I'm doing this is because it's the last thing on this earth I can do for the one who helped me so much of my life."

Suddenly I was transported back in time to when I was about four. Momma was standing beside me as I looked in the mirror in the bathroom while getting dressed for the day.

"Let me help you comb the back of your hair; you have a cowlick, and it is standing up. I am proud of how nice you dressed yourself. You even matched your colors. What a big boy you are today," she praised me. Even before I could do it myself, Momma protected me by building my pride and self-worth.

I thought I was having an actual conversation with Momma. I said, "I want to see that your hair, make-up, and clothes for going out of this world are just right." I moved closer to the faucet and began turning the device on to the proper temperature and pressure. I didn't want the water too hot or too cold, and I didn't want it to spatter back onto her face. I tried to imagine this as a simple hair washing bowl that I had used hundreds of time before. Our conversation started again.

The color was now mixed. I put cream around the hairline so it would not distort and leave a line of demarcation. By coloring the hair through to the ends of her hair, the entire hair strands got the same amount of new color exposure. I looked down to see the coloring of the hair had taken from the scalp to the ends of her hair. It had. We continued our conversation.

"Momma, I don't know if any of us ever told you how much you were needed. I wish your life had not been so hard. You deserved better. You did without, so we could have more," I said softly, almost crying.

Suddenly I thought of Momma fussing over me as I finished dressing for my eighth-grade graduation. She was making sure my white shirt, dark pants, sweater (borrowed from an older brother), and tie that she found at the thrift store were clean and pressed.

"Many people in town think because we are poor and not educated, that graduating isn't important. I know this graduation is not going to be the last one for you. I plan to be there with you when you graduate from high school too. I don't bet, but if I did, I would bet anyone that you are not only going to college, but you will graduate," Momma predicted.

"People can think what they want. They don't control us. I promise you Momma; I'm going to go to high school and college and graduate from both. I will make it. I am going to become either a preacher or a teacher and help others who need help because you have given me the desire to succeed. You taught me to have the courage to dream. You have always said for me to believe in myself. I do! I will!" I responded with confidence.

Momma had me look directly into the mirror. She said, "Repeat after me, I am not ashamed of who I am; but I won't be a farm worker when I grow up."

I turned from the mirror and looked at Momma, "Is there anything wrong with me wanting to get out of this place? I don't know where I'm going to go; only that I have to go someplace else," I said, as I looked at what I thought was Momma four years ago.

She answered, "I know your father wants you to quit school and finish raising the girls. You can't. The social workers won't allow you to be responsible for them. Follow your dreams, your desires, the inward feelings that no one else sees."

I looked down at the slab where Momma lay. Her hair was now one even color. It was time to style her hair. I set her hair with rollers. I used medium sized rollers so I would have plenty of movement for styling purposes. As I worked to complete this task, I continued my conversation with her.

"Momma, I have one thing people can't take away. That's me. I won't be the brightest student when I get to college. Yet, I can take the knowledge that will be provided to me and make the most of it," I explained.

Momma smiled and said, "I know your desire is to help people, all kinds of people. When it is your turn to go, people will say 'he did so much with so little.' "When you gain fame always be quick to give your teachers the credit for all of your accomplishments; they saw your potential when so many questioned it."

When Momma finished speaking, I realized I was back in the mortuary using a teasing comb and smoothing her bangs from the right side of Momma's face to the left side; the side she preferred. I admired how much better she looked from when I had started. Her true beauty was almost complete. I said, "I'll miss that you won't be able to sing to me anymore."

"I will be able to hear you sing whether it is in private, in a church, or on television; your message will be positive, accepting of others, and always willing to listen to find an acceptable solution," she sang in an Indian type of chant instead of speaking.

Immediately I was back in the room finishing the final touches on Momma's hair. I was glad Momma was beyond pain and suffering.

The manager returned. I was relieved that another person had joined me in the room as I finished Momma's hair styling. I asked the manager to help me with her make-up. We worked together to make sure the application looked very natural. Momma did not need much blush, eye liner, or lipstick to accent her natural attributes.

The last thing we did was to dress Momma. We moved her body from the workstation to the coffin. I learned a secret about dressing the dead that day. The clothes that are used for the coffin are split open in the back so they can be tucked under the body. By doing this, any dress, jacket, shirt, pant, or vest can be made to fit. We finished and I looked at the red dress we had given Momma on that wonderful Christmas a few years earlier; it looked even prettier on her than it had in the box when she opened it. She had never worn it before.

Once I was out of the room, I had to sit down. I had no energy left.

CHAPTER TWELVE

The funeral was scheduled for Friday and, of course, it rained. The chapel was too small for all of those who had come to pay their respects. Some of the mourners were forced to stand outside because there was not enough room for them inside. During the service three of my older sisters demonstrated untypical behavior. They were yelling, sobbing, and my sister, Hannah, actually fainted and her husband had to attend to her. My brothers-in-law were trying to console them; but, to no avail. As the minister delivered his message, utterances were made aloud by the family, relatives, and friends, which filled the room and reminded me of a Pentecostal revival meeting.

"Momma, I love you," shouted one sister.

"Why did you have to go?" asked another.

"It's just not fair," cried someone else.

"Come back, Momma!" petitioned more than one of my siblings.

All of these utterances were made in love, concern, and appreciation for the love Momma had provided to so many. They were made because of the lives she had touched during her time on earth. One never knows how many lives one effects throughout a lifetime. During the ceremony, I sat thinking of the various people who had passed through my life. I tried to think what it would have been like if I had not met that person. Would I have learned that particular lesson from anyone else? I began thinking what I might have learned had I been born in another family.

As my family passed by the coffin, each member was touched in a different way. I realized that while I had been watching Momma lying in bed at the hospital so close to death, I had held a ray of hope for her healing. As long as a person is capable of breathing, there is the possibility of a miracle. I wanted to see her recover. Every time she made what I interpreted as an improvement, I thought that perhaps God was making the miracle of healing come true for her.

What I did not realize at the time was that the miracle may, in fact, be the passing of our loved one; so that he or she experiences no more pain. I also knew that I did not want to remember Momma in a coffin. I wanted to remember her alive, full of caring and understanding. I wanted to remember her healthy. I wanted to remember the moments she looked after me.

Father, Hannah, Karen, Frances, Donald, and I were seated in the family car as we drove to the cemetery. No words were uttered. I looked at Father. He too had been crying. He had not shared with any of us any reason for his behavior. He had not said anything to us that would show his concern for how we felt. There were simply no words from him at all.

I wanted to give him the benefit of a doubt. His wife of over thirty years was gone. The woman who had helped him make many of his important decisions was no longer going to be there to give advice. I felt his conduct for the past year had been to simply cover-up his inability to face the fact he was losing the woman who had loved him through the worst times, had stood by his side during financial disaster, and had held his hand during medical emergencies. Perhaps his terrible loss would give him greater compassion for those around him.

The cemetery was wet and cold. The wind was blowing directly into our faces as we made our way to the graveside. It wasn't just sprinkling. The clouds seemed to open up and pour buckets of water right on top of where we were standing. None of us had umbrellas. In fact, we did not even have heavy raincoats. Friends from my church were carrying Momma to that last resting place her physical body would ever know.

Pastor DeWolfe had asked for volunteers to act as pallbearers. I was impressed and proud of these men, who had taken off work to show support for me and for Momma. Inside that box lay the body of the woman responsible for whatever I was going to become. There would be no more guidance chats, no more inquiring about the birds and bees; there would be no more looking into one another's eyes to search for truth.

The graveside service did not last very long. I remember Pastor asking if anyone would like to take an opportunity to say something. I don't remember anyone speaking. I have been told a couple of people spoke, but I have no memory of that happening. I do remember how cold Karen and Frances were. They were hugging each other for warmth. I remember getting between them and embracing them.

I was glad we had gotten Momma a nice coffin. The owner of the funeral home was a friend of Pastor DeWolfe. I promised him if he would guarantee the amount of money, we were short to buy the coffin, I would be responsible for the cost and pay it back to him in monthly payments. He agreed and I made monthly payments to him until he was reimbursed. One of the coffins they had shown us was a pine box that looked like it had been made from plywood and appeared to be very flimsy. When the dirt tumbled on top of the coffin we bought, it would not give way. Momma would have a secure resting place.

Father had picked a headstone out from a catalogue, but he did not have enough money to pay for it. None of the older kids had extra money to lend him. The cemetery informed us that Momma would have a small marker with her name on it, which would identify her burial spot for those who wanted to visit her grave, until a permanent headstone was installed. Father told them he would pay monthly payments until the headstone was paid in full. It could not be ordered until the final payment was received. I know Father never made any payments, because in 1973, I paid for her headstone.

The next memory I have was when we were driving away from the cemetery. The same family car brought us back to my former home in silence. As I stepped onto the porch, I heard Hannah and Jasper, and their three-year old son, getting out of their car. Her husband Jasper was in the Army and had been given a special pass so that he could come to the funeral from Georgia, where he was stationed.

My two little sisters sat dejected on the sofa, each girl holding the other's hand. My twin tried to act unmoved as he stood on the north end of the room, skimming through a book. He never read. Father sat with his head bowed and his eyes closed. For the first time this day, he gave outward signs that appeared genuinely hurt. Hannah, Jasper, and their son came through the door one after the other in military marching style. From my own vantage point, in the bedroom doorway, I saw a last desperate attempt by them to try and ease the loss that each one of us was experiencing.

"Up, two, three, four. Up two, three, four," they said, entering the house. Hannah stopped first. She looked around the room anxiously. Her eyes were swollen, red, and moist. "Momma is better off. I just know she is," she said. Hannah looked at the two girls. "You know, we can't be selfish today. We all loved Momma, and we want her to be here now; but what happened was really the best for her." Hannah spoke softly as she moved toward the girls.

Father raised his head and opened his eyes. Suddenly his eyes were not full of deception, but rather, there appeared love never seen before nor since. His eyes were wide, his face full, firm, and very precise. He began to speak to his own children, products of a love gone forever. "I really loved yar Ma; she was probly the most giving woman that ever existed," he said. Each of Father's children were stunned; they listened respectfully.

"Yar Ma and me, we had a good life together. Ain't always been happy, but life ain't always full of roses. I been hearin ya kids cryin and weepin and sayin how ya miss her. But, ain't none of ya goin miss her more than me. We ain't never had much, but we always shared what we made together. It wasn't real nice, some years, when I had nothin to give her for her birthday, or for Christmas, or even on our anniversary. None of ya know what it's like not to give the woman ya love nice things. The older kids got it better than us, and ya four smaller kids got it better than they had. Yar Ma and me worked out in them old fields, sweatin, hoein, and shovelin the ground to raise yones the best we knowed how. I know ya don't think I can hurt, but yar wrong. When we didn't have any money or food, and them bill collectors was comin here, or callin and waitin for their money. She was always there with me.

After ya kids'd go away or go to bed, she'd take hold of my hands and she'd put em up to her face, and then she'd kiss em real soft and then she'd pull me close, real close to her; and kiss this old ugly cheek of mine right here, just below my eyes," he said. He looked at each of us for just a second, and then, like a professional speaker, focused his eye contact to include all of the audience in the room as he continued. I didn't quite understand the last few sentences he uttered. Something did not ring true.

"She would always say it's O.K. We're gonna make it. And then she would smile that real pretty smile that would make her eyes light up. I'm gonna miss that closeness. We've slept in the same bed every night since we been married; except for those nights she was in the hospital. Now that she's gone, that bed's gonna be lonely. Yer Ma ain't gonna be there to get me up each mornin or to go grocery shoppin or be there for cleanin the house. She ain't gonna smile at me ever again. Ya kids lost a Ma. I lost my wife. I lost the woman who was the mother of all you children. I lost the only real friend I ever had," he admitted. If Father was acting, he was as good as one could be. If he was telling the truth, his vulnerability was being exposed to all who would care to listen.

"I ain't sayin this to get ya to fill sorry for me. I want ya to know yer not the only ones who is hurtin today," he said. I could tell each of us felt some type of shame for what we had thought, or had allowed ourselves to imagine, these past months concerning him. We had thought only of ourselves. We had failed to realize Father had not lost his mother; but, rather, his bride of over thirty years. He had each one of us exactly where he wanted us. We were willing to give him another pass towards forgiveness. This was a side of him none of us had seen. The sensitivity that he showed appeared to be sincere, caring, raw, and truthful.

As if given a cue by a director, we all moved toward Father. As we reached out to touch him; he stood up and pushed us away. He went to the center of the room, making him the dominant actor on stage. He was now the center of attention. "Now, I want ya kids to sit down cause we got some talkin to do. The older kids don't matter. You all married and on your own. Ronald, ya ain't here in the home. Ya say you gonna go off to college. I don't know why. The other boys ain't needed as much learnin as you already got, but that ain't none of my business anymore cause ya ain't livin here at my home anymore. Donald is in the Navy. Now that leaves ya two girls. I know ya think yar big and grown up, but ya ain't," he said. Father was beginning to take the conversation to the place he wanted when he was staging this entire performance.

"Now, I ain't the kinda man that's gonna throw ya out. I just hope ya can make it here with me. I'll do my best. I'd like to say I can get off work early and be here when ya get home from skool in the afternoon. But, I work long hours; sometimes twelve, thirteen, fourteen hours a day. Ya got to anymore just to make ends meet. I can't see that yoons are takin care of. They gonna be days when you gonna be here by yerselves after skool and late into the nite," he said.

I saw Hannah look at her husband and he nodded. She turned to face each of us. She crossed her hands as she interrupted, "Daddy, Jasper and I talked and, well, since I lived here at home most all my life, except for the past four years, we think the girls are at an age when they need a woman around the house. We don't make a whole lot in the service, but we're willing, we want, to finish raising the girls. Don't we honey?" she asked her husband.

Jasper nodded approvingly and then spoke to the two girls. "We know we can't replace either your father or your mother. We wouldn't want to do that. However, you girls would have Hannah to talk with and to be a mother image," he said. Momentarily, Father looked elated. For just an instant, I saw a short quick smile. He exhaled heavily. His body seemed to gain new energy and vigor. Just as fast he turned back into the depressed and beaten-up mourner; he appeared very solemn.

"I thank ya for the offer. But I guess will just have to try to make it, unless ya girls want to leave here and go with Hannah," he responded tactfully. My sisters were being asked to choose between their father and their sister. If they stayed, there would be many lonely nights and days, more alcoholic encounters, and no mother to protect them. Hannah had always been a second mother to the girls.

Karen spoke up first, "Daddy, what do you want us to do? Are you gonna be home at nights with us? Are we gonna have to worry about you night after night?" she asked.

Hannah interrupted. "Daddy, I think it would be best if I took the girls. You don't have any objections to whether we will watch out for them properly, do you?" she asked. The question that none of the older kids really wanted to ask had been spoken. She was actually asking for permission to remove the two girls from his custody. Father had arrived at the moment his entire performance had built toward.

"Well, guess it'd be O.K. If none of the rest of ya don't care. I do have some fear. Now, Hannah, I hope ya don't think this bad of me, or take it the wrong way, but I been told Jasper has tried things with the girls," he said. He paused to see what kind of reaction his statement had on all of the family listening to him. Hannah was furious at this accusation. The rest of us were stunned.

Hannah shouted, "What are you saying? You think Jasper has done something with these two little girls?" she asked.

"I never used them words. I never said he did. Jest rumor has it that he tried to," Father said.

"Rumor? Daddy what are you saying? You can't just drop something like that out and not expect a reaction. Jasper has to go on trial right here, right now. Let's get all of this out in the open! He is standing right here in front of you. Ask him if it is true?" she demanded.

"I problee never should have brot it up. I am sorry. Let's forget it," Father seemed to be backing down, but Hannah would not let him.

"If you won't ask him or the girls, I will. Karen and Frances, has Jasper ever touched or done anything to you that is improper?" Hannah asked. The girls had already faced what many children never experience by losing a parent in death at such an early age. Now they were experiencing another traumatic moment. Both were very sad, but empathetic with their responses.

"No!" said Frances.

"Absolutely not!" said Karen.

Jasper spoke next. "Bill, I have tried to stay out of this as much as possible. I told Hannah she could do whatever she wanted. She loved her mother very much. I even told her I would help her finish raising the girls because I thought it would help you and the girls. However, I resent what you are implying. I want to know from you who told you that. I can be court marshalled and be cast out of the service if something like this were to be true," he added. Jasper's voice was raging mad. Father sat back in his chair smiling.

"I don't see the big problem here. I mean, we settled this thing didn't we? You say ya didn't and I believe ya," Father said as he smiled again at the end of his sentence.

"No Bill, this is not so simple," Jasper was not satisfied. "I want to find out who said something so cruel because it is going to surface again unless we put an end to it. Now, who said it?"

"I don't really remember. Now, what have ya girls decided to do? Ya going to stay with me and get along as best we can, or are you going with Hannah and Jasper?" he asked.

Hannah moved between Father and her husband. "Daddy, do you know how bad something like this can look if it is repeated by others. My husband could get kicked out of the Army. He only has six more years before he can retire. My own children could wind up hating their Father, if this is not cleared up. It can cause trouble between us. Now, who said it? Who said it?" she screamed.

I did not believe what my eyes were seeing, nor my ears were hearing. We had been subjected to one of the most draining events of life (the loss of a mother) and now we were in the middle of a small war. Father clenched his fists. He again moved toward the center of the room.

"Well, if ya have to know, I think it was Ronald who told me," he said. I didn't think I heard correctly. All eyes turned on me. Hannah and Jasper came closer as Father returned and reclined in his chair.

"Wait! Wait, just one minute," I spoke. But, before I could continue, a scuffle ensued, and my brother-in-law caught me with a right punch to the head that knocked me to the floor.

"Jasper!" my sister Hannah screamed.

"Ronald!" shouted Karen.

"Stop!" yelled Frances.

I pulled myself to my feet and pointed my finger at Jasper.

"Don't you touch me again! Do you hear me? I will file a charge against you for aggravated assault and you will face a trial. I no more told him anything like that than...," I said as Hannah interrupted.

"Ronald, what is going on with our family?" she asked.

"Stop it. All of you just shut up and wait a minute. I don't know why Father just told that lie, but I suppose there is a reason. Father, do you want to explain why you said that about Jasper and the girls and blamed me for such a lie? Why lie today of all days?" I pleaded. Father rose to his feet and raised his arm back ready to fight anyone who dared to question him.

"You been deservin this beatin a long time and its caught up with ya today," he shouted at the top of his lungs and looked directly at me.

"Father, you better remember what I told you at the hospital. I am not going to ever let you run over me again. You are going to be shocked when I defend myself. If you hit me this time, I am going to hit you back for every single time you hit me in the past when I did not deserve it because I had not done anything wrong," I said. Suddenly it dawned on me why Father had started this nasty rumor. I turned and looked directly at Frances and Karen.

"Girls, I wish I could stay here and take care of you. I don't want to be separated from you; but I already talked to the welfare department and they say I am too young to be responsible for three of us."

Frances spoke up, "But we don't want to stay with Daddy if you aren't here. Who will go and get him at night when he is drunk?"

Karen had another idea, "It would be best if we all three could stay together and not be split up. Is there any way the three of us can be together?"

Frances tried one more time to keep us together. "Is there anybody who is willing to take the three of us as a package? Ron can help with the expenses because he works all the time. Karen and I can get some kind of after school job. We won't be much of a burden," she pleaded. It was heartbreaking to hear Frances trying to convince one of her siblings to add three more to their already growing households.

I had to speak, "You know what, Father? Earlier when you were talking about loving our mother, you almost had me convinced you were telling the truth. But your willingness to lie about me persuades me that Hannah and Jasper can take care of the girls better than you ever could. I never said anything bad about him. But you know what, Father, it almost worked for you. Listen, all of you, if Father can get us fighting among ourselves, and if you, Hannah, take the girls to raise, he gets exactly what he really wants. What he really wants is his freedom from all of us; freedom from his family," I said.

Jasper moved toward me again. This time he was not angry. "Ron, I am so sorry for hitting you. I just lost it when I heard you might be responsible for that vicious rumor." I accepted his apology.

"Father asked me not to live at home anymore. I didn't want to leave. He didn't want me. I think your exact words were, 'Get out of my home' weren't they, Father? So, you are going to get your request. I am leaving. This is just a house. There is no home here." As I looked at all the family members, I thought to myself, one day, I too will have my own family. I am going to love that family with all my heart. My children will be told they are important, told they can become anything they wish, told that love means accepting people for who they are and not what we want them to become."

Hannah interrupted me, "I knew in my heart that you would not say anything like that about Jasper. I have never heard you lie about anything, unlike someone else in this room whose name I could mention."

I had one last thing to say to Father. "It doesn't surprise me that your bed is the only empty thing you are going to have that you will miss. I am sure it won't be empty long. But what will be empty for a very long time is the fact you are not going to have the love of your children. Someday you are going to want us, or need us, and I just hope there will be enough love and understanding left for you by all of us; even me, when you need it." I left the house.

I had one last duty to perform for Momma. I drove to the hospital where Momma had received such good care during those months that preceded her death. I took a dozen red roses and left them for the nurses who worked on the sixth floor. I attached a card that read, "Thank you for taking care of our mother. One red rose from each of her ten children, one from her husband, and one from Momma, even though she is no longer with us."

CHAPTER THIRTEEN

That was Friday. On Monday morning, thinking that Father would be at work, I stopped at his house. I was on my way to cosmetology school and wanted to pick up the last few items I had left behind. I think I really wanted to sit and reminisce about Momma, who had been very much alive while we lived here as a family. I entered the living room and a peculiar feeling came over me. This was no longer a home. It was merely a house where a family once lived, fought, cried, laughed, and loved.

I heard a noise coming from my parents' bedroom. I felt a bit anxious, but then I heard Father's laugh. Not even two days had passed since we put Momma in the grave. The door opened. I looked expectantly. A woman stood in front of me, with a towel over her shoulder, a sheet wrapped around her body, her hair ruffled, and a cigarette in her hand. Father stood there in his underwear.

"Hi there! Do you know us? Billy, do you know this person out in the living room?" she asked. Father looked directly at me.

"Ronald, boy, what ya doin here? I thought you was supposed to be gone. Did I not make it clear to ya about not comin around here?" he asked.

"I just came by to pick up the rest of my things," I said. I could not help looking at the two of them. They had been caught in a moment of lust. This was a moment of desperation for a man who only wanted sexual gratification.

"Billy is this one of our sons? He is kinda cute!" said the Blue Moon Lady. Yes, it was the same lady from the Blue Moon bar.

"Yeah, he's one of the twins. Remember, ya met him before at the Blue Moon," Father reminded her. I had nothing to say, so I turned to leave. But, as I changed direction, she decided to step forward. I thought she was still intoxicated. I did not want to know how long they had been drinking. She started to fall forward. Father tried to help her. His condition was not much better than hers. She recovered a little bit, but she stumbled backwards; he fell forward. They both were trying to stabilize each other. If this had been any other situation, it might have been funny. For an instant, I felt sorry for both of them. It didn't make sense to me that she could be with him so soon. She knew his wife had just been put to rest. She tried to smile. "We haven't been here long. I just came by this morning to clean up the mess for Billy. I was just going to go bathe. Your Dad is a good man. I can't take the place of your Mom right now, but which one of my new sons are you again?" she asked. The fact that Momma wasn't even three days buried, and that Father had deliberately torn the family apart so he could have his freedom wasn't sitting well with me. I could feel anger beginning to rise from the bottom of my feet working its way through my body and out of my mouth. I looked directly into her eyes. I chose my words very carefully and deliberately.

"Miss, and I use that word with great caution. You are not my mother. You will never be my mother. I would prefer that you not call yourself my 'mother' in my presence," I said as I turned to face off with Father.

"You are not my father; not anymore. Most men can biologically conceive a child. I remember hearing you say that all you were doing when I was conceived was just having fun. But being a father is how one raises and supports a child. I want to thank you for having me, for giving me the opportunity to live; even though I wasn't planned. I also want to thank you for working in the fields twelve hours a day, seven days a week, while I was growing up. I appreciate the fact that even though you couldn't read or write, you never let us starve; you always provided for us. Finally, I want to thank you for marrying Momma and making a family for the first eighteen years of my life. I will always appreciate that dedication. But since Momma got sick with cancer, and you started drinking and doing exactly what you are doing this morning; you stopped being my father. You won't be my father again until you stop being so selfish and being concerned only with your own physical needs. I don't know what you have become, but I don't like it and I don't want to be around it," I said.

They began to giggle. She moved toward him and kissed him. Both stood before me kissing. He looked over at me. "So, what am I now, boy?" he asked. I turned to leave. I did not need any of the material things I had still in that house.

"What am I? I am happy, that's what I am!" Father claimed.

"This is not true happiness. This is anything but happiness. This is disgusting. I am glad the girls are not here to see this. It was the best thing for them to leave you. Right now, you are not a good father. You are not a good husband who just lost his wife." I didn't know what he was to me at that moment.

"You are only the man who was having fun that resulted in my being born," I said as I moved closer to the open door.

I closed the door to the Park Lane house and never returned to what was once my home. By the time I got to and mounted my motorcycle, my eyes were full of tears. They were streaming down my cheeks and my entire body trembled. I had to put the past, which I could not change, behind me; and I had to face forward with courage and determination to the next chapter in my life.

I decided to drive to the one place I always felt safe; I drove to Pastor DeWolfe's home. I wanted to share with him just how much more my life had been turned upside down. Just when I thought no additional pressure or disappointment could be asked of me, Father's betrayal hit me like no other illness or obstacle to that point in my life.

As I approached the DeWolfe home, I noticed familiar faces assembled in the front yard. Friends were carrying packing boxes; some had big rolls of tape, and others were carrying empty boxes already assembled. It looked like a "moving party." A senior church official saw me and said, "Pastor is in his office at the church, I think you should go see him now." I turned the bike around and headed to the church.

I saw Pastor's car and another car, which I did not recognize, in the parking lot. I went to the side entry and knocked on his door. I heard Pastor say, "Come in." I entered. Pastor saw it was me and said, "Ron, I am so glad you are here. I wanted to find some time last week to meet with you to share some exciting news; but with all that was going on in both our lives, I did not find the opportune time." He turned to the gentleman sitting at his desk and said, "This is Pastor David Kennedy."

I smiled and responded, "Nice to meet you." I asked Pastor DeWolfe, "Can we talk when you are free?"

"Of course. Pastor Kennedy and I have just completed his orientation meeting. I will be free in a minute or two." I walked back to the parking lot. I thought about his words, "orientation meeting." Our church was not large enough to support two ministers. We averaged about ninety-five people each week and about fifty more for special services like Christmas and Easter. There had been talk of opening a God's Holy Assembly in Clovis. Perhaps Pastor Kennedy had been selected for that post.

The church office door opened and both men walked out. Pastor Kennedy said, "Thanks for the insights. I'll see you back at your house." Pastor DeWolfe motioned for me to return with him to his office.

"Is he a new local pastor?" I asked.

"Yes! He is going to be my replacement here. Now that Larry has finished college, I have decided to go back and finish my teaching credential and begin teaching. We are going to move to the Northridge area of Los Angeles while I work on a secondary credential and a master's degree at the same time. We came here thinking we would stay a couple of years and it turned out to be ten. Just think, you and I will be in college at the same time."

I was not going to spoil his celebration by telling him about my problems. My solid, stable, unwavering rock was moving. Instead, I smiled and said, "You have always talked about going back to school.

You must be very excited. When you begin teaching; your students will be so lucky. When are you moving?" I asked.

"By the end of the week," he exclaimed.

"That is wonderful; but it doesn't give you much time."

"Did you want something from me?" asked Pastor DeWolfe.

"Oh, I was just going to set a date for me to return your bike to you."

"How is Thursday?"

"I can make that happen."

"Why don't you come here on Thursday around noon. Pastor Kennedy and I are going to meet at 11:00 a.m. and I want him to know more about you and why I have been and will always be supportive of you as a person, Christian, and a soon to be positive influence of our society," he said. I told him that I would love to meet with the two of them.

The past month had been so out of control, I had not followed through with committing to any of the three colleges to which Mrs. Huckleberry had helped me gain entry. By Wednesday, I found that only USC was still available to me. Trinity University, my first choice, informed me when I called them that because I had not responded by their deadline, they had given my place to someone else. They were full and had a waiting list. I could not imagine going to live by myself in the Los Angeles area. College was to start in two weeks, and I needed to act; and act fast.

When I came back to see Pastor DeWolfe and Pastor Kennedy on Thursday, I heard them praying. I stood at the door and listened to them; they were praying for me.

"Father, bless Ron and put your hand of protection over him as he journeys into college life," I heard Pastor Kennedy pray.

Pastor DeWolfe added, "Heavenly Father, Ron has been through so much during his young life. Reward him and make his dream of escaping from this area and way of life his family knows, become a reality. Give him the strength and courage to become the light you want him to be, helping him become a "Fisher of Men" and bring many to know you though him."

I knocked on the door and was invited into a room that was full of love and good will. We talked about some of my experiences growing up. Each step of the conversation was led by Pastor DeWolfe who complimented me on how well I had conducted myself. Finally, I shared with them my colossal blunder concerning enrollment at Trinity.

Pastor Kennedy spoke, "I may be able to help. Dr. Billingsley, the President of Trinity and I are friends. Let's call him and see if he can make this mountain move." He took out a business card from his wallet and called a number.

"This is David Kennedy, is Dr. Billingsley available?" There was a pause. "Thanks for taking my call. How are things going?" There was a longer pause in the conversation. "As you may know, I am here with Pastor DeWolfe in Clovis, California. We have a very special young man who applied and was accepted to attend Trinity, but within the last six months, he has lost both his mother and his father. He did not get all of his paperwork back to your college in time. Is there any way I can call in a favor and have him admitted for the fall semester?"

Again, there was silence for what seemed like minutes. "His name is Ronald Reel," he said, and more silence filled the room. "God bless you. I understand. His scholarship and student loan will be waiting for him! He will be there by the end of the week. Thank you so much."

POSTSCRIPT

1968 - 2025

This is a synopsis of what I have done from the time I entered my first true college, Bethany Bible College, until the present.

Education:

School & Location	Year(s)	Degree
Bethany Bible College, Scotts Valley, CA	1968-1969	
San Joaquin Delta College, Stockton, CA	1969	
Bakersfield Junior College, Bakersfield, CA	1970-1971	AA
California State University Fresno, Fresno, CA	1971-1973	BA
California State University Fresno, Fresno, CA	1973-1974	MA
Pacific College, Fresno, CA	1974	Secondary Teaching Credential
University of Southern California	1975-1976	
Valley Christian University, Fresno, CA	1975-1976	Ph.D.

Azusa Pacific University, Azusa, CA	1978	Administrative Credential
Southern Baptist Convention, Covina, CA	1982	Ordained Minister
California Appraisal School	1997	Licensed
California Real Estate License	1998	Salesperson
California Real Estate License	2000	Broker
National Mortgage School	2000	Licensed Agent
Oregon Real Estate License	2013	Principal Broker

Employment:

Part-Time

Tinkler Mission Chapel

Numerous hair salons, restaurants, paper mill

California State University, Fresno

Full-Time

Job	Title	Year(s)
Bakersfield Junior College	Director of Forensics	1974-1976
Bakersfield High School	English/Forensics	1976-1979
New Life Christian Fresno	English/Forensics	1980-1981
Clovis High School	Forensics	1981-1983
Covina Christian Elementary, Covina, CA	Vice Principal	1983-1984
South Hills Academy	Principal	1984-1985
Goddard Junior High School, Glendora, CA	English	1985-1986

Ron Reel Ministries	Owner	1985-Present
Cal Poly, Pomona, CA	Assistant Director of Forensics	1986-1987
Mt San Antonio College, Walnut, CA	Speech/Director of Forensics	1984-2013
Long Beach Real Estate	Salesperson	1998-2000
Reel Properties, Covina, CA	Owner	2000-2006
Reel Mortgage, Covina, CA	Owner	2000-2005
Aloha Pizza Company, Los Angeles	Owner	2003-2005
Century 21 Agate Realty, Brookings OR	Broker	2013-2014
Pacific Ocean Properties, Brookings, OR	Owner	2014-2021
Pacific Ocean Properties, Crescent City, CA	Owner	2018-2021
Ron Reel, Author	Owner	2019-Present
Premier Ocean Properties, Brookings, OR	Owner	2021-Present
Reel Properties, Crescent City, CA	Owner	2018-Present
Reel Properties, Long Beach, CA	Owner	2023-Present

Personal

I arrived at Bethany Bible College in Scotts Valley, California, with all my worldly possessions, consisting of four shirts, two pairs of pants, two pairs of shoes, underwear, toothbrush, deodorant, aftershave, pen, pencils, a ream of lined paper, and my Bible. One of my three roommates was named Rich, and I thought he was. When he moved into our room, he filled his closet quickly, opened my closet, saw it was almost empty, and asked if he could use it as well. I agreed under one condition; I could wear anything housed in my closet. During the year, many young ladies commented on how Rich and I had similar taste in clothes.

I left Bethany at the end of the academic year for a summer job in Antioch, California, where my brother Joe got me a job running chemical tests on paper pulp at the paper mill where he worked. This same summer Aunt Alma and Uncle Skip asked me to live with them, and they eventually adopted me.

Because of my decision to live with them, I left Bethany and transferred to San Joaquin Delta College in Stockton, California. I decided on a drama major and speech minor. I participated in plays and joined the competitive speech team. Father showed up in September of that same year; and rather than living near him, I moved back to Bakersfield to live with my sister Nellie and her husband Leo. Once again, Leo helped me purchase a car and I enrolled at Bakersfield College, where I successfully competed in the state and national junior college tournaments.

During the summer I had an opportunity to take a four-week course in argumentation at California State University, Fullerton. I wanted to learn how to debate and Dr. Lucy Keele was one of the premier debate coaches in the state. I drove from Bakersfield to Fullerton three days a week. I had never spent much time in such a populated area and felt unprepared to finish my college experience in such a crowded place. I told Dr. Keele about my fears and she recommended that I consider a less populated area that had a good university with a growing reputation in competitive debate. She suggested I visit California State University,

Fresno, and meet their new coach, who was already making a name for himself, Dr. Hal Bochin.

I drove to Fresno, met with Dr. Bochin, heard what type of program he envisioned (strong in debate and individual events), and decided it held promise for me. I met with the Fresno financial aid office and secured a grant and loan combination. I would have no family or other financial assistance once I moved to Fresno. Early in my first semester I had not eaten for a couple days and went to the Fresno County welfare department. Who knew that you had to wait two weeks while they verified your need for assistance? The kind parents of another debater, Mr. and Mrs. Robert Weatherson, heard of my plight and moved me into their home for almost a year.

My three years at Fresno were the most life-changing time of my life. I was challenged academically, and I established a lucrative hair business. I made some lifelong friends; I excelled in speech competition, but most importantly, I found myself. After finishing my bachelor's degree, it was a no brainer to stay on for a master's degree.

I returned to Bakersfield to teach at Bakersfield College and Bakersfield High School so that my federal loans would be forgiven and paid in full. During my time in Bakersfield, I sent students to the state and national finals, giving them the same experiences, I had received. I continued to travel back to Fresno on weekends while I handled twenty to twenty-five hair appointments to supplement my income. I left Fresno in 1979 and moved back to Antioch. During the year I reflected on what was important to me as I made plans to go forward.

In 1980 I moved back to Fresno, accepting a teaching and coaching position at New Life Christian High School. I assembled an incredible group of students who far exceeded my expectations in term of awards won and willingness to work. Unfortunately, the senior pastor of the church and school made a million-dollar investing mistake and the school closed without notice and without paying the faculty.

Because of the success of that one-year program, I was offered a full-time job at one of the most prestigious schools in Los Angeles as well as one at Clovis High School, in the Fresno area. It was a very hard decision. I felt it was time for me to leave the valley for good, but two of my very best students could transfer to Clovis if I chose it. I accepted the job in Clovis and found to my delight that Pastor Earl Gould had accepted a job as student counselor there. After an exciting year and half in Clovis I had a chance to move up in school administration, starting as a vice principal in Covina, California. The following year I progressed to a principal job. I took a one-year job as a junior high teacher before landing at Cal Poly, Pomona, as assistant debate coach. We did well but the department decided to discontinue the competitive program. This turned out to be a blessing in disguise for it resulted in my finding my dream job.

Mt. San Antonio College, the largest single campus community college in California, advertised for a speech position that included starting a forensics program. I applied and got the job. During the next twenty-five years, I would not only direct one of the most successful forensics programs in the United States, but I would serve as department chair for twelve years. I co-authored a textbook, *From Fright to Might*. All royalties from book sales go to the speech team. I created, produced, and directed a scholarship show at Mt. San Antonio called *Puttin' on the Hits* where professors, staff, administrators, trustee members, and students performed lip sync routines of the greatest entertainers. That annual show has raised hundreds of thousands of dollars for student scholarships.

Starting as the local president of the Community College Faculty Association, I became the state-wide union treasurer, vice president, and became the first president to serve three consecutive terms.

During these years, in addition to me teaching full-time, I began a successful real estate and mortgage company. Along the way, I owned eight restaurants. Due to the malfeasance of a business partner, who raised the ire of the IRS, the business collapsed, and I ended up owing more than I owned to the federal government. I had to file for bankruptcy. Eventually all my debts were satisfied.

In 2013 I retired from teaching and became a full-time resident of Brookings, Oregon. I began again. I worked for Century 21 Agate Reality for one year and then went out on my own with Pacific Ocean Properties in Brookings and eventually Reel Properties in Crescent City, California. I also own a real estate management company, caring for rental properties, condo associations, storage facilities, and vacation rentals along the Pacific coast. I have spent the last six years working very hard and God has blessed me with financial success.

This book has given me the opportunity to share in depth the first eighteen years of my life to see the obstacles I faced and how I overcame them. I hope my success will inspire you and I hope you read the two additional memories that continue this journey.

www.ingramcontent.com/pod-product-compliance
Lightning Source LLC
Chambersburg PA
CBHW020448130626
46549CB00001B/343